THE SOUTH'S NEW RACIAL POLITICS

"Glen Browder's analysis of biracial leadership in the modern-day South is a significant contribution to those seeking to understand the relationship between blacks and whites in the political arena. It provides key insight into how black and white leaders, once at polar extremes of the social and political spectrum, have forged a working relationship that attempts to provide public policies that will benefit their respective constituencies. He does not gloss over the division of the Old South, nor does he paint a picture that all is well in the New South. He lays out a thesis that biracial accommodation exists and that the South is better off as a result of it."

> — Dr. Artemesia Stanberry, North Carolina Central University

"Glen Browder's work is informed by his academic perspective and by his experience as a politician and public official. It's an unusual combination and it makes for insight that one does not get much from the political science discipline. Anyone interested in understanding contemporary southern political dynamics should start with him."

> — Dr. James M. Glaser, Tufts University

"In dealing with this topic, Browder brings to the table the very rare combination of insights stemming from his lengthy record as an academic and political practitioner. The interface between race and politics in the American South is a complex one that, on occasion, has been simplified by writers with either an ideological bias or limited insight. The topic certainly deserves additional treatment since it ultimately undergirds the region's longstanding distinctiveness."

> — Dr. Jess Brown, Athens State University

THE SOUTH'S NEW RACIAL POLITICS

THE SOUTH'S NEW RACIAL POLITICS

INSIDE THE RACE GAME OF SOUTHERN HISTORY

GLEN BROWDER

NewSouth Books
Montgomery | Louisville

NewSouth Books
105 South Court Street
Montgomery, AL 36104

Copyright © 2009 by Glen Browder.
All rights reserved under International and Pan-American Copyright Conventions.
Published in the United States by NewSouth Books,
a division of NewSouth, Inc., Montgomery, Alabama.

Browder, Glen.
The South's new racial politics : inside the race game of southern political history / Glen Browder.
p. cm.
Includes bibliographical references and index.
ISBN-13: 978-1-60306-050-9
ISBN-10: 1-60306-050-2
1. Southern States—History. 2. Southern States—Politics and government. 3. Southern States—
Race relations. 4. African Americans—Southern States—History. 5. African Americans—Southern
States—Politics and government. I. Title.
F209.B76 2009
305.800975—dc22

2009011908

Printed in the United States of America

To Becky and Jenny

Contents

Author's Note

Through mutual permissions, this book shares some excerpts, factual presentations, and political observations with two other titles forthcoming from NewSouth Books: *Professor-Politician* by Geni Certain with Glen Browder, and *Stealth Reconstruction: The Untold Story of Southern Political History* by Glen Browder in collaboration with Artemesia Stanberry. I am grateful to Ms. Certain, Dr. Stanberry, and NewSouth Books for the use of this material.

The present manuscript is part essay, part history, part political science—and mainly original. Since it is essentially an interpretive commentary, I'll use footnotes where I think they add something interesting and helpful or necessary—not just to "academicize" the manuscript.

I

Introduction

A T HIS 1963 INAUGURATION in Montgomery, Governor George C. Wallace pledged racial defiance forever in the Heart of Dixie:

> In the name of the greatest people that have ever trod this earth, I draw the line in the dust and toss the gauntlet before the feet of tyranny . . . and I say . . . segregation today . . . segregation tomorrow . . . segregation forever.[1]

A few short months later, in his "I Have A Dream" speech in Washington, Dr. Martin Luther King articulated an alternate vision of Southern race relations:

> I have a dream that one day the state of Alabama, with its vicious racists, with its governor having his lips dripping with the words of interposition and nullification, will be transformed into a situation where little black boys and black girls will be able to join hands with little white boys and white girls and walk together as sisters and brothers.[2]

Neither of these guys—the two most prominent men in Southern racial history—had a clue back then about how Alabama and the South would look a half-century later. Little did Wallace and King know that, as I will illustrate, both races would embrace ironic and un-visionary accommodations in the twenty-first century.

King was killed by an assassin's bullet five years after his "Dream" speech;

so he never saw the fruits of his labor. Wallace was shot and paralyzed a decade after his inaugural remarks about "segregation forever"; he died years later, a changed politician and repentant man grieving about his role in history and history books.

So, what would I tell Wallace and King about Alabama and the South if somehow I could communicate with them today? How would I explain— from my privileged perspective and position inside Southern politics—about where we are now? And how we got here?

Sadly, I would have to admit to them that racism extends into the new century. But mainly I would relate an intriguing story of evolving Southern politics. That story—as told in this book—is that the South has changed considerably since the civil rights movement; and in many respects, this region now practices an ironic but somewhat normalizing version of national politics.

AN ORIGINAL THESIS OF THE SOUTHERN RACE GAME

In this original analysis, I will talk about race—the most essential and difficult aspect of Southern history—and the race game that Southerners still play as part of their historical legacy.[3]

Frankly, I know the Southern race game inside and out! I have been around Southern politics—as a native Southerner, political scientist, and public official—since the days of Dr. King and Governor Wallace. I have studied and played the game with the best and the worst of the race-gamers—white and black—for decades. I can attest that it is an intriguing, enduring, ugly anomaly in the "Great Experiment" of American democracy.[4]

The South has always been different because of its "peculiarity"—or more accurately, its stubborn racial practices in a nation that subscribes to the self-evident truth that all people are "created equal" and whose children regularly pledge "liberty and justice for all." This region has maintained its distinctive, peculiar ways through slavery, segregation, and discrimination— even into the twenty-first century.

The white leaders and people of this region historically engaged in a race game designed to provide themselves the blessings of democracy while oppressing, exploiting, and discriminating against their fellow human beings of African origin and heritage. For many, it was simply the Southern way of life that they were born into and never seriously deliberated or morally questioned; but, at its core and in its effect—as practiced by cynical officials, ambitious politicians, and everyday citizens—it constituted a perverse, contorted, racist system.

However, today's racial politics seems to be a different and somewhat surprising story of biracial accommodation, as evidenced in its substance, style, strategies, operations, and outcomes. I believe that Southern politics has evolved into a qualitatively distinct regime in the twenty-first century; and I offer my thesis as the first theoretical conceptualization and practical interpretation of this new system of racial politics in the South.[5]

I first conceived my version of Southern "race-gaming" as a political science professor consulting on election campaigns in the 1970s; I discovered the practice of biracial gaming as an elected official in the 1980s and 1990s; and I developed my game-theory of white-black accommodation—the "New Racial Politics"—as a professor-turned-politician-returned-to-academia in the early years of the twenty-first century.

This background convinced me that we must probe the Southern race game more creatively and less normatively than in the past. We must consider new ideas, alternative explanations, and the actual politics of changing Southern history. Thus, I will now focus on some relatively ignored but important developments in the race game of Southern history.

An Unusual Analysis of Real Southern Politics

This will be an unusual analysis of "real Southern politics"; i.e., the raw racial conflicts, trade-offs, alliances, and transactions, both out front and behind the scenes, that have underlain the Southern race game for the past half-century.[6]

It may seem strange to imply that "real politics" has been slighted in normal coverage of the South; but to a degree that has been the case. Scholars and journalists have filled libraries worldwide with useful, interesting books and articles about race and Southern political history; but it is hard to find anything that documents or explains the actual, essential, base racial politicking that is usually hidden in the back rooms and in the hearts and minds of white and black leaders in this region. Public officials don't normally like to talk about such sensitive matters as white-versus-black contention; journalists love the race conflict but aren't interested in the practicalities of making democracy work; and academics, whether interested or not, generally don't have inside knowledge about racial politics and government. "Real Southern politics" indeed happened and is still happening in ways that are uniquely regional and systemically important; and this story merits consideration in standard assessments of politics in the South.

I concluded early in my career that campaigning and governing were tough assignments anytime and anywhere. But dealing successfully with the challenges of politics and policy-making was different and difficult—and often impossible—in a Southern society fundamentally racked with racial legacies of the past and relentlessly pressed forward by powerful forces of change.

White rule had always pervaded Southern politics, as a "given" and without a lot of fanfare; but the civil rights revolution changed all of that. White-black issues thereafter challenged and disrupted every aspect of the Southern way of life. Southern politics assumed a different nature in the latter half of the century, out of necessity to accommodate new realities.

Subsequent politicking could be just as raw as before, but it was different in several respects. First, both whites and blacks had to participate together in politics and government for the first time since Reconstruction. Second, they both knew that they had to start resolving issues of fundamental importance to their antagonistic constituencies. Third, both sides had to conduct themselves in at least some accord with federal rules, laws, and oversight. Finally, and just as importantly, for obvious political reasons, these biracial interactions quite often had to assume discrete manners, strange procedures, and racialized outcomes unprecedented in this region and unknown and misunderstood in the rest of the country. Thus, if "real Southern politics" was traditionally peculiar, it became hyper-peculiar—white dominance mixed with racial affirmative action—in the post-civil rights movement period.

Race was not simply another factor in the political process—it was the central reality that altered and confounded the entire political arena after the movement. Documenting the nature and activities of this central reality is critical in understanding Southern politics, and thus far I have found no satisfactory assessment of this aspect of recent Southern history.

I don't think my academic and political colleagues from other parts of the country ever understand when Southern politicos—black and white alike—talk about their strange relationships, racial confrontations, and biracial accommodations in Alabama and other parts of the South. But, then, they never experienced "real Southern politics."

A DIFFERENT APPROACH TO SOUTHERN POLITICAL HISTORY

My focus on the "race game" and "real politics" differs significantly from conventional accounts of Southern politics since the civil rights movement.[7]

Most professional analysts of Southern political history have based their assessments on personal interviews, written documents, and statistical studies. I draw from my involvement as a participant-observer, so this will be a new, authoritative, inside look at the difficult, elusive interactions and dealings among white and black politicos since the civil rights movement. In addition to relying on my academic credentials as a long-time political scientist, I will tackle important questions and developments that have been exaggerated, overlooked, or avoided—for a variety of theoretical, methodological, and normative reasons—in the mainstream literature.

Next, I want to emphasize what this book is not.

Clearly, this manuscript is not a standard history or government textbook. There's no pretense of rigorous objectivity or methodology. I write what I know from my background as a professor-politician, intermingling scholarly research and political insights and experiences as they fit my purpose. Conventional texts and articles on this period can be found elsewhere.[8]

Also, this is not a comprehensive recitation of more obvious aspects of recent Southern history—i.e., continuing civil rights conflict, grudging civil rights progress, black voter registration, the election of black officials, white partisan shifting, the development of a two-party system, and the "reddening" of Southern elections. Accordingly, I make no claim that my commentary is the most important or only acceptable version of what has happened and is happening in the South. My analysis is one approach that

I bring to the table of Southern political discourse. Of course, I contend that the "race game" and "real Southern politics" are central to understanding the South. I'm convinced that it is impossible to comprehend Southern history without tangling with white-black issues and relations deep in the belly of the Southern political beast.

As a final aside, I'll dispense with modesty and say that I also think my account is a timely contribution to the contemporary public discussion of racial politics and history. In this analysis, I question common conceptions of regional intransigence, and I will suggest that perhaps President Barack Obama should conduct his national dialogue on race here in the South.

ACKNOWLEDGING MY BACKGROUND AND OTHER ISSUES

I should post up front a few acknowledgments.

First, I'm a native white Southerner immersed academically and politically in Southern history. In addition to my primary calling as a political scientist from the 1970s to the present, I served in public office as a Democrat in Montgomery and Washington for much of the 1980s and 1990s; and I was a party activist/campaign consultant intermittently during that era. My twin careers in academics and public service generally focused on practical reform and civic progress. I recognize the possible impact of my personal background, and the reader should factor that background into this analysis.[9]

Second, some may take issue with my blunt language about sensitive, serious matters. The central aspect of my analysis—"race-gaming"—could be interpreted as callous, impolitic reference to what for many individuals was and is still a painful experience. My insider talk about "real Southern politics" might sound arrogant and self-serving to some readers. Rest assured, I do not intend to be callous or arrogant. But I have been blessed to both study and practice politics at fundamental junctures of time and events in this region, and I wrote this book to break new ground in analysis of Southern politics. My participant-observer status has well positioned me to expand, clarify, and flesh out the narrative commonly communicated in textbooks, journals, biographies, and the news media; and the language used in this book conveys appropriate emphasis on important developments that are either missing from or exaggerated in conventional accounts of Southern political history. I believe that my work—including the rhetorical dramatics of my terminology—fairly complements mainstream Southern history.

Third, I should acknowledge that some of my ideas will be even more controversial than my terminology. The book will anger some native politicians who don't like my digging up old political bones. It will probably bother many others—whites and blacks, Southerners and non-Southerners, liberals and conservatives, academics and journalists—because of my interpretation of Southern race relations of the past and present. And it may puzzle outsiders trying to make sense of this part of the country. But this book is an honest effort to depict Southern political history more fully and accurately than has been the case in the past; and I look forward to discussions with those who disagree or don't understand my commentary.

So this is my story of the race game and real Southern politics since the civil rights movement. Or, to be more precise, this is my rendition of the evolving South—from the "Old South," through "Southern Democracy," and into the "New Racial Politics"—as I have observed and experienced these developments in my conjoined career as a professor-politician.

Now, before considering evolutionary politics, let's talk about the overarching race game and real politics of Southern history.

II

The Race Game of Southern Political History

I BEGIN MY ANALYSIS by discussing something that academicians and journalists can only speculate about and that most politicians don't like to admit—the cynical race game of Southern political history.

THE RACE GAME AND REAL SOUTHERN POLITICS

Scholars and the news media have amply chronicled the civil rights movement in the South; and most Americans now speak reverently about Dr. King, Rosa Parks, the Freedom Riders, and other heroes of the dramatic revolution that rocked the region a half-century ago. Also seared into our collective conscience and consciousness is the memory of the South's massive resistance to that revolution. Images of Southern white racism are still vivid and often brutal: Governor Wallace standing in the schoolhouse door, Bull Connor and his police dogs, ugly crowds at Little Rock, the Birmingham bombings, the Orangeburg Massacre, and Bloody Sunday.[10]

However, America seems to have little sense of how that public struggle among heroes and villains during the 1950s and 1960s actually played into Southern politics from the 1970s on into the twenty-first century. It is clear that race and racism continue as powerful forces in the contemporary South; but, just as clearly, scholars have not sufficiently explored—theoretically and empirically—the causal nature and biracial pattern of the evolving race game as practiced in this region. In fact, few analysts understand that a new racial order—a politics of open, candid, biracial accommodation—now prevails throughout much of the South.

The race game itself is really quite simple. Ever since their colonial beginnings, the white leaders and people of this region have engaged in perverse, contorted politics designed to provide themselves the blessings of democracy at the expense of black Southerners. Gaming the system for racial advantage was not the singular, continuous, consuming passion for most Southerners; but slavery had warped the Southern political system from the start, and race forever lurked in the background of Southern political life.

This race game has been a source of curiosity and contention throughout our country's history. It has demeaned black Southerners, white Southerners, and Americans everywhere. It absolutely contradicts the "Great Experiment" of American democracy. It provokes worldwide calumny. It endlessly fascinates scholars and the news media. But perhaps the most striking aspect of the game is its stubborn durability over time.[11]

As might be expected, most white Southerners today disavow the race game, and they probably don't think that they personally have ever gamed the system for racial advantage. Furthermore, the legal framework of segregation and discrimination no longer exists. However, the game persists because of de facto legacies—demographic patterns, cultural differences, economic disparities, and simply bad racial feelings.

I generalize that most Southern political leaders—both white and black, past and present—have played the race game in some manner and to some degree. Few ever talk about it with family, friends, or neighbors, and it's not a popular subject at commencement ceremonies or on the civic circuit. But the routine pursuit of power, policies, and other political goodies in this region has always involved racial considerations and practices.

This is not to suggest that the race game is a uniquely Southern way of doing things. It is obvious that race is a complex, sensitive issue; and politics is politics—or "who gets what"—whether in Montgomery or Washington or Boston or Sacramento. In national campaigns for the U.S. presidency, for example, Republicans schedule photo ops with black celebrities and Democrats emphasize their cultural empathy (and in some cases their "blackness") for the African American community; and big-city politics in other sections of the country often involves intense racial and ethnic dealings.

Nor am I implying that racial deliberation in campaigns and public service is, in itself, morally wrong. In a way, candor and directness in racial matters have been healthy developments in overcoming historical racism. I simply am acknowledging that race-gaming has been prevalent and intense due to the lingering history and volatile context of Southern politics.

We all should note, however, that real Southern politics changed dramatically—in ways that have yet to be fully explored and analyzed—after the civil rights movement. Although race had always been an acknowledged and prominent part of Southern politics, racial politicking assumed different nature and heightened consequence as the two races were thrown together, under federal oversight, to deal with difficult issues and antagonistic constituencies, in the post-movement period.

Real Southern politics thereafter became hyper-peculiar. Southern elections—whether for the local school board or the U.S. Senate—became a minefield of racial volatility, as reported in painful detail by the national media. Less noticed but equally excruciating was the fact that all policies and functions of governance—education, health care, welfare, justice, transportation, agriculture, environment, national defense, social issues, moral causes, taxing, budgeting, grants, appointments, constituency service, everything—turned into testy racial wrangling at every stage of the process. While whites usually enjoyed majority control, blacks countervailed through cohesive tactics, federal mandates, and judicial oversight. The two races waged constant warfare, even on nonracial matters; and more often than not, the result was gridlock for many years after the movement. Ironically, however, the South emerged in relative calm and routine order—still with racial tensions but with a new game of biracial accommodation—in the new century.

In this chapter, I will first lay out the historical background and systemic dysfunction of Southern politics, as commonly depicted by scholars and journalists. I will secondly demonstrate, citing some of those same sources, that the South has changed dramatically in more recent times. The intriguing follow-up, then, is explaining, more specifically, the what, why, and how of this change. And what does this tell us about the course of Southern politics? In later chapters, I will provide some of the answers through my unusual analysis—"real Southern politics" inside the "race game"—of evolving Southern political history.

HISTORICAL FOUNDATIONS OF REGIONAL RACIAL DYSFUNCTION

In some ways, the South can claim to be the original, intellectual heart of the "Great Experiment" of American democracy, and many Southerners pride themselves as America's real and true patriots. However, from the beginning, the South steered its own regional course, a distinct culture of white supremacy in an America that at least preached idealistic principles of equality.

The unsavory realities of Southern politics derive from an anomalous, flawed, accursed aspect of the American story. In embracing slavery so adamantly, this part of the New World launched long-term, systemic developments that would confound its better nature and democratic destiny. The South thence pursued its dark regional interests in fateful arrangements—and perhaps implicit collusion—with national politicians eager to promote their nationalistic dreams.

CONSTITUTIONAL ORIGINS OF A "PECULIAR" POLITICAL SYSTEM

During the Constitutional period, there was contentious debate over slavery, but the Southern states persuaded founding fathers to accommodate the regional slave economy as part of their entry into the new nation. Senator John C. Calhoun of South Carolina proudly defended the so-called "peculiar institution of the South" as "a positive good"—constitutionally, historically, politically, and morally—on the floor of Congress in 1837.[12] Even after the Civil War and Reconstruction, states throughout the region continued Old South ways by legally disenfranchising blacks. As Alabama's constitutional convention president said in 1901, "it is within the limits imposed by the Federal Constitution, to establish white supremacy in this state."[13]

Southerners thus were able to negotiate an opportunistic new deal that excluded blacks from the political process as long as the South delivered total electoral support to the national Democrats. Regional white rule continued until the civil rights era, when the national government finally eliminated de jure discrimination. The South thereafter shifted to more informal maneuverings—which I cover in this essay—to maintain the Southern way of life.

Unfortunately, then, throughout most of its history, the South's political system revolved around the realities of white supremacy and racial segregation. While Southern leaders historically pursued broad issues of national and local import, racial factors routinely influenced the conduct of politics and government, to the obvious satisfaction of their white constituents. The pertinent reality of Southern political history has been a cumulative, combustible race game combining democracy with black-white tensions in a conservative society of overlapping class and caste and a stubborn political leadership coupled with irresponsible electoral and party systems, all within a regional hothouse of entrenched dysfunction and a national pattern of historical accommodation. As a result, the South has forgone rational debate about normal, substantive issues of American democracy for most of its history; instead, it has diffused its energies in a troubling continuum of racial contention.

THE FUNDAMENTAL FLAW OF SOUTHERN POLITICS

According to political scientist V. O. Key Jr.—a native Texan and perhaps the most insightful analyst of Southern politics at that time—the fundamental flaw of Southern history has been a systemic failure of Southern leaders and political parties to address conjoined problems of race and poverty.[14] As he so famously articulated the thesis in *Southern Politics in State and Nation* (1949):

> When all the exceptions are considered, when all the justifications are made, and when all the invidious comparisons are drawn, those of the South and those who love the South are left with the cold, hard fact that the South as a whole has developed no system or practice of political organization and leadership adequate to cope with its problems.[15]

Key accurately stated a daunting challenge for Southern political leaders:

Obviously, the conversion of the South into a democracy in the sense that the mass of people vote and have a hand in their governance poses one of the most staggering tasks for statesmanship in the western world. The suffrage problems of the South can claim a closer kinship with those of India, of South Africa, or of the Dutch East Indies than with those of, say, Minnesota. Political leadership in the State of New York or California or Ohio simmers down to matters of the rankest simplicity alongside those that must be dealt with in Georgia or Mississippi or Alabama.[16]

Thus, at the midpoint of the twentieth century, before the days of Wallace or King, "Southern politics" essentially meant "white Southern politics." African Americans were nonexistent in most discussions. Mainstream analysis of the time fretted about whether whites could ever be persuaded to accept Negro participation in governance (or how Negroes could force themselves into the democratic process). Systemic dysfunction engendered harsh racial politics throughout the region; and few foresaw a biracial course for addressing the Southern rendition of an American dilemma.

AN INTRACTABLE DIVIDE BETWEEN WHITES AND BLACKS

Even as the civil rights movement intensified, expert analysts sometimes despaired of success because of the South's intractable segregation and dysfunctional leadership.

Donald R. Matthews and James W. Prothro, after extensively and statistically portraying both sides of the region's populace in *Negroes and the New Southern Politics* (1966), worried about the future of regional democracy.[17] They even referenced the possibility of a racial holocaust:

> In the South today the white leader who contemplates a tentative step toward accommodating Negro demands can expect to be labeled a "nigger-lover"; the Negro who cooperates with white leaders can expect to be labeled an "Uncle Tom." Indeed, we seriously wonder whether a viable political system in the South will be possible, granted the extreme polarization of opinion, without one race being dominated by the other.[18]

Although civil rights leaders, grassroots demonstrators, and the federal government scored effective assaults on the Southern way of life, political developments during those times reflected a worsening racial situation and suggested dismal prospects for bringing blacks and whites together.

In their depiction of Southern politics and society of the late 1960s, Earl Black and Merle Black articulated the situation thusly:[19]

> The changing civil rights agenda, widespread white opposition to significant reforms concerning the intermediate color line, and the new black militancy had profound consequences for the major civil rights organizations . . .
>
> Just as black Southerners were beginning to participate in electoral politics in significant numbers, prospects appeared remote for successful biracial coalitions built upon issues of central concern to blacks. In no Southern state were there enough white allies to support a winning liberal politics, much less a radical politics.[20]

Indeed, the civil rights movement played out in the 1950s and 1960s as a protracted civil war between advancing blacks and retrenching whites (with most leaders siding with their core constituencies), rather than a successful resolution of the South's historical dilemma; and there was very little hope for meaningfully reconstructing the Southern political system.

Furthermore—despite the United States government's having weighed in with the *Brown* decision, the Civil Rights Act, the Voting Rights Act, the National Guard, and federal registrars/pollwatchers—as the 1960s drew to a close the national environment for black causes was regressing and there was little hope for a new brand of Southern leadership.

In recounting that era, Richard K. Scher systematically listed the problems of the declining movement:[21]

> The civil rights movement continued after Selma and the passage of the Voting Rights Act. It continues to this day. But after 1965, it was never quite the same again, for a number of reasons.

In the first place, it was a victim of its own success. . . . Next the focus
of the civil rights movement shifted. . . . Vietnam and its accompanying
turmoil began to take over the nation's headlines. . . . Related to these
concerns was the growing white backlash. . . . Finally, the civil rights
movement itself became irrevocably split. . . . As a result, the direction of
the civil rights movement because confused, diffused, uncertain.[22]

As for the possibility of biracial leadership, Scher noted that "some former
allies of the movement joined the increasingly shrill black militants, while
others became disenchanted and felt that the movement neither wanted nor
deserved white support. By the late 1960s and early 1970s, it was almost
impossible to tell what civil rights leaders, and the black community—
Southern and otherwise—really wanted."[23]

William R. Keech, who studied varying impacts of voting and other
political actions in Southern communities of that time, speculated that the
problems of blacks perhaps were unfixable through electoral democracy
(1968):[24]

The real problem is much deeper than these tactical considerations
imply. The tragedy of American racial history is that it has left the Negro
with more problems than men of good-will are able to solve. Votes, litigation and even the threat of violence are useful because they can influence
the behavior of elected policy-makers. The most frustrating problem of
the American Negro in politics is that even if elected policy-makers were
totally responsive to Negro demands, it is not at all clear that they have
it in their power to eliminate the inequality with which three and a half
centuries of discrimination have saddled the American Negro.[25]

Thus, apparently, the concerns of early analysts about biracial politics
were well-founded; and the heroic struggle seemed to be running out of
steam.

BUT THE SOUTH DID CHANGE ITS RACIAL WAYS AND POLITICS

Surprisingly, however, the South changed. Despite several centuries of entrenched racism and biracial electoral disasters of the 1960s, regional politics began evolving in different manner in the 1970s. Some may debate the merits of the subsequent pace and direction of Southern politics, but the South began—haltingly and stubbornly and constantly pressed by civil rights groups and the U.S. Justice Department—to address its historical dilemma.

Notably, scholars have documented substantial moderation, convergence, normalization, and transformation of the South during the post-movement period. According to scores of social scientists, Southern politics has progressed dramatically through demographic change, cultural moderation, civil rights litigation, black empowerment, and partisan developments.[26]

Earl Black and Merle Black, for example, cited both partisan and racial aspects of "reformed" Southern politics in *The Rise of Southern Republicans* (2002):[27]

> The old Southern politics was transparently undemocratic and thoroughly racist. "Southern political institutions," as V. O. Key Jr. demonstrated, were deliberately constructed to subordinate "the Negro population and, externally, to block threatened interferences from the outside with the local arrangements." By protecting white supremacy, Southern Democrats in Congress institutionalized massive racial injustice for generations. Eventually the civil rights movement challenged the South's racial status quo and inspired a national political climate in which Southern Democratic senators could no longer kill civil rights legislation. Led by President Lyndon B. Johnson of Texas, overwhelming majorities of northern Democrats and northern Republicans united to enact the Civil Rights Act of 1964 and the Voting Rights Act of 1965. Landmark federal intervention reformed Southern race relations and helped destabilize the traditional one-party system. In the fullness of time the Democratic Party's supremacy gave way to genuinely competitive two-party politics.[28]

Charles S. Bullock and Mark J. Rozell similarly summarized these developments in *The New Politics of the Old South: An Introduction to Southern Politics* (2007):[29]

When V. O. Key (1949) published *Southern Politics*, the region was solidly Democratic. No Republican had been elected U.S. senator or governor in decades, and a generation had passed since a Republican collected a single Electoral College vote. For most of a century after Reconstruction, the South provided the foundation on which the national Democratic Party rested. When the party was in eclipse in the rest of the country, little more than the Southern foundation could be seen. During periods of Democratic control of the presidency and Congress, as in the New Deal era, the South made a major contribution. After the 2004 election, the Democratic Party in the South had been reduced to its weakest position in more than 130 years. Today Republicans win the bulk of the white vote, dominate the South's presidential and congressional elections and control half the state legislative chambers.[30]

Furthermore, they noted, the South's racial situation evolved dramatically.

Key's South had an electorate in which Republicans were rare and blacks even scarcer. While he observed that "in its grand outlines the politics of the South revolves around the position of the Negro," it was not a commentary on black political influence, which was non-existent, but rather an acknowledgment that the region expended much political capital to keep African Americans away from the levers of power. Since implementation of the 1965 Voting Rights Act, black votes have become the mainstay of the Democratic Party—the vote without which few Democrats can win statewide. The votes cast by African Americans have helped elect a black governor (Virginia's Douglas Wilder), eighteen members of Congress and hundreds of legislators and local officials.

Partisan change and black mobilization have not been continuous but have come at different paces in various locales and for different offices. Nonetheless, the changes have been massive.[31]

Additionally, journalists have begun depicting a different, more positive vision of Southerners in terms of racial ideas and behavior.[32]

John Fleming, a native white Alabamian and editor-at-large of the *Anniston Star*, spends considerable time exploring and writing about the South; he painted a similar picture of civil and subtle change in the hard-core Deep South.[33] After several days in Selma, for example, he said that the struggle for black political empowerment has been won; the city has a black mayor and a majority-black city council. He also described contemporary race relations there as complex, forever evolving, never clear-cut, but worth studying by and for the rest of America.

> Today, traveling up U.S. 80 from Montgomery, along the route of the historic march, past the sprawling fields and pastures of the Black Belt, across the bridge and into town, one finds an immeasurably more peaceful Selma. It's a more civil and subtle place.[34]

Race is still at the heart of the town known as the cradle of racial intolerance, according to Fleming: "It bubbles below the surface; its undercurrents touch nearly every aspect of life." But he reported that steady progress has been made since the 1960s.

> Then, people of authority and those of the street spat the utterances of racism into the faces of fellow humans. Worse, people died for seeking equality and for helping others to achieve it.
>
> In today's Selma—a place that carries a heavy burden for the injustices and for the behavior of some of its citizens so long ago and that sticks in the consciousness of the nation as a marker of an unacceptable level of inhumanity—a sort of racial healing seems to be taking place among a festering that in many ways can be a lesson to the rest of the world.[35]

It is not my intent to cover the scholarly and journalistic literature here; I simply note that there is overwhelming evidence and sentiment that the Southern political system has shifted significantly toward the normal practices of broader American democracy.

PERSONAL TESTIMONIALS FROM BLACK SOUTHERNERS

Just as telling as statistics and news reports, and inherently more interesting, are the personal stories of civil rights icons asserting that things have changed in the South. The following remarks of native Alabamians demonstrate imperfect but responsive change, and a certain sense of personal pride, in the new Southern politics. Perhaps it's a function of their age, but these Southern black leaders aren't dwelling on confrontational strategies or electoral triumphs of the past; now they seem more focused on improvements in black-white relations and the "Southern way of life."

The most ironic testimony comes from John Lewis, now a Georgia congressman, a Selma-to-Montgomery marcher who was beaten on Edmund Pettus Bridge, and a former Freedom Rider whose family still lives in Alabama. Lewis articulated a strong message of positive change in his biography, *Walking with the Wind: A Memoir of the Movement* (1998):[36]

> No one, but no one, who was born in America forty or fifty or sixty
> years ago and who grew up and came through what I came through, who
> witnessed the changes I witnessed, can possibly say that America is not
> a far better place than it was. We live in a different country than the one
> I grew up in. The South is different. . . . So many things are better. . . .
> There is no denying the distance we have come.[37]

Fred Gray, attorney for Dr. King and Mrs. Parks and a giant of the Alabama civil rights movement, focused on legal changes in his biography, *Bus Ride to Justice: Changing the System by the System* (1995):[38]

> I have watched the appellate courts in Alabama in recent years, par-
> ticularly the Alabama Supreme Court. In my opinion, we now have a
> court that demonstrates respect for the constitution and laws of not only
> the State of Alabama but also the United States of America. I feel very
> comfortable in appearing before our appellate courts and arguing state
> law questions or federal constitutional issues, and I feel that the courts
> will rule on the issues in accordance with the law, regardless of the parties
> and regardless of race, creed or national origin. . . .

Power has been utilized in the movement to change society from total segregation to one which is becoming ever more just. We are not there yet, but we are moving in that direction. I believe that the success of the legal cases that I have been involved in speaks well for democracy and for the Constitution. It shows that one can use the system, abide by its rules and regulations, and change society.[39]

Similar positive and personal reflections were expressed by the late J. L. Chestnut Jr., a Selma native and respected pioneer of Alabama's civil rights battles, in concluding his biography, *Black in Selma: The Uncommon Life of J. L Chestnut, Jr.* (Chestnut and Cass 1990):[40]

On the ride home from Opelika that Martin Luther King's birthday, though, I felt pretty good. I slowly crossed the Edmund Pettus Bridge at sunset. There was Selma. The *Times-Journal.* City Hall. Our law firm. I reflected back on my return to Selma on the same road in 1958. From the vantage point of how things used to be, the present is not so discouraging. When I stop and look back, I see the many barriers that have fallen and the great distance we have traveled. Remember, I started out thinking we'd be making substantial progress if we could just get a string of black-owned supermarkets in the Black Belt. It's disappointing that we don't have them, but, in context, this was a modest goal. We've gone beyond where I even dared imagine—black people and white people.

I see my own life as helping to realize the dream in my world in Alabama. Though I never imagined I'd spend my whole life in little Selma, I don't know of a better place I could have taken a stand. Selma is my home. I love Selma. It's my life.[41]

These three pioneers of the movement qualified their statements appropriately, but such comments are dramatic endorsements of Southern change.

"WE AIN'T WHAT WE WAS"

These pronouncements of significant advancement in Alabama—from reputable Southern scholars and from inside the black community itself—echo the conclusion of an outsider who studied Mississippi politics, comparatively, first in the 1960s and then again in the 1990s. University of Illinois political scientist Frederick Wirt had captured the early, daunting challenge of the movement in the Deep South; he returned for follow-up research toward the end of the century. Wirt reported remarkable change in *"We Ain't What We Was": Civil Rights in the New South* (1997):

> The combination of new economic development, new civil rights laws that opened voting to blacks, new movement of population, and new ideas about an improved political system—all combined to create a New South that observers agree is unprecedented. No one thinks that this change is complete, for blacks complain about needs that are still unmet. But it is equally clear that an understanding of the region's politics must go beyond what V. O. Key once knew and what national opinion once held. There is now a new political system with changes still under way.[42]

Race and racism are still vital matters, and much remains to be done; but, as this review of academic research and personal testimony has clearly demonstrated, the South changed dramatically between 1950 and 2000.

EXPLORING THE EVOLUTION OF SOUTHERN POLITICAL HISTORY SINCE THE CIVIL RIGHTS MOVEMENT

How did the South get from "what we was" in the Old South to substantial racial progress of the twenty-first century? Equally importantly, what does the answer tell us about the race game of future Southern politics?

This assignment would seem an easy task. However, it does not take much time at the library or on the computer to discover that there has been little work on inside, routine, black-white politics over the last few decades, and what we can ascertain is piecemeal, oblique, and perplexing.

We find, as has been noted in the preceding pages, flourishing statistical analysis of many aspects of the emergent South, such as shifting social and economic patterns, moderating cultural parameters, the expanding role of African Americans, and rising Republicanism in Southern public life. We find many sweeping generalizations, interesting historical narratives, and solid legal reports—flush with names, events, places, and dates—describing important developments. There are fascinating anecdotes touching on changed race relations. Interspersed throughout are periodic reports qualifying our notion of progress, reports that testify to the continuing problem of white-versus-black in this part of the country.

These analyses provide a vast literature describing, inferring, and speculating about Southern change from 1950 to 2000. But something important is missing from the conventional story line on racial politics of the last few decades: there's no satisfactory accounting of real-world political transactions that comprise the dynamic nature, substance, and process of systemic change. In particular, there is nothing in the literature that addresses—theoretically, comprehensively, and coherently—the inside "what" and "how" and "why" of political progress that has occurred in Southern politics since the contentious days of the heroic drama.

Obviously, the civil rights movement endures as a dominant phenomenon and analytic concept of twentieth-century American democracy. Its heroes deserve full credit for their moral suasion, personal sacrifices, and righteous triumphs in fighting for equal rights and racial justice during the 1950–60s. However, I think that it is highly unlikely that the movement, by itself, wrought subsequent, substantial transformation by heroically and dramatically hammering Old South politicos into progressive submission. In many ways, the days of protest, violence, and forced desegregation were somewhat like the Civil War experience, leaving white Southerners whipped and resentful, and unleashing bad memories and fresh grievances among black Southerners. Furthermore, that ordeal afflicted all with an uncertain, distrustful future. Progressive politicians and civil rights leaders faced formidable obstacles in nurturing biracial relations and racial progress in such an environment; their antagonists (including white segregationists and black separatists) certainly were disinterested in forming partnerships for progress. Consequently, the heroes constantly struggled against recalcitrant villains, resistant populations, and traditional practices in the Southern states, and thus the Second Reconstruction waned considerably during the late 1960s and early 1970s, again just as had happened with Civil War Reconstruction a century earlier. But, somehow, inexplicably, the monolithic struggle of good-versus-evil morphed into a relatively normalized political system by 2000.

My point is that the stark Old South did not embrace progress simply through the heroic drama of the civil rights movement; and there has been little accounting for critical, causal developments in the evolving race game of a new and different South.

Thus the nagging retrospective assignment recurs—i.e., logically squaring this important incongruity of Southern political history. How did we get from the Old South to the New Racial Politics? Or, to slightly re-state the intriguing question: "What really happened—inside the belly of the beast—between then and now?"

Much of the answer obviously lies in the evolving race game of the past half-century; so let's take a look inside "Southern Democracy."

III

The Rise and Fall of Southern Democracy

IN THIS CHAPTER, I will assess dramatic change in the Southern race game by examining "Southern Democracy," a regime of traditional political culture that ruled the region during and after the civil rights movement. I will attempt to demonstrate that the "race game" evolved quietly and fundamentally under this regime and during this period; I also hope to demonstrate that "real Southern politics" contributed substantially to that evolution.

SOUTHERN DEMOCRACY: A FRIENDLY BUT FATED REFUGE

As I use the term, "Southern Democracy" refers to the white South's frantic attempt to defend trumpeted principles—such as "states' rights"—and preserve its cherished way of life—"segregation forever"—under growing attack from the federal government and the civil rights revolution.[43] During the latter half of the century, Southern Democracy would prove to be a friendly but fated refuge for the white South.

Just as they had done a century before, hot-blooded Southern whites rallied en masse against inevitable change during the 1950s and 1960s. This time, however, they ensconced their rebellion in the political institution that had served them well since Reconstruction days—their peculiar version of the Democratic Party and its network of partisans throughout the region.

Such resistance was not surprising to Southern historians and rabid defenders of the Lost Cause. From the Civil War through the middle of the twentieth century, regional white supremacy and segregation had reigned without question, due in great part, as I have already stated, to the corrupt gentlemen's agreement with national party leaders and tight suppression of Southern blacks. As Earl Black and Merle Black have written:

> For generations after the Civil War, Southern political leaders invested all of their political capital in the Democratic Party and leveraged their influence in that party on behalf of the practices and institutions of Southern racism.[44]

But after World War II, this coalition between national liberals and regional conservatives began to deteriorate; and progressive forces outside and inside began chipping away at the Southern monolith. President Truman's integration of the military (1947) and the Supreme Court's rulings against the white primary (1944) and segregated education (1954) put the white South on notice that change was coming. Then followed widespread, disruptive, direct action by native blacks—like the Montgomery bus boycott (1955), sit-ins (1960), freedom rides (1961), mass demonstrations (1962–63), and voter registration campaigns (1964–65)—along with the Civil Rights Act (1964) and the Voting Rights Act (1965).

Southern whites embarked on a course of siege resistance, committing their society, politics, and government solidly against the forces of change; and the various state party organizations served that commitment very well, providing a veil of legitimacy and effective suppression of newly enfranchised black voters in the Old Confederacy. Thus Southern Democracy prevailed during and beyond the movement.[45]

White one-party rule during that era was simply an evolved version of Old South politics: a renewed, enhanced regime of segregation in the face of unprecedented internal and external assault. Southern Democracy worked effectively, for a while. But the various racist parties declined to uncertain, tentative, diminished stature during subsequent decades. In the 1950s, Old South Democrats had succeeded in massive resistance to the rights revolution; in the 1960s, they voted almost lock-step for defenders of the Southern way of life; in the 1970s, their resistance began to waver in some areas; in the 1980s, they experienced serious identity crisis throughout the region; and in the 1990s, many Democrats—even with newly embraced black voters—were routed by Republicans. By the end of the century, Southern Democracy was an embarrassing memory.

I will not dwell on the civil rights movement, which is covered in countless other sources. But Southern Democracy serves as an appropriate backdrop for my account of the race game and real Southern politics. Southern Democracy was the most prominent, dominant, functioning political regime between 1950–2000; and its course accurately reveals the South's intense racial resolve and, over time, the region's abandonment of traditional ways.

On a personal note, I never engaged politically during my young years and I missed the early, fiery dramatics of the civil rights movement and Southern Democracy. However, upon earning my PhD in political science from Emory University in 1971, I plopped down in a front-row seat at Jacksonville State University in Alabama, from where I was able to study and observe first-hand the dark spectacle of traditional race-gaming. Then, beginning in the late 1970s, I crossed over into politics, working as a campaign consultant, political party activist, Alabama state legislator, Alabama secretary of state, and U.S. congressman. So, I base my analysis on both academic background and political experience.[46]

TRADITIONAL MALPRACTICES OF SOUTHERN DEMOCRATIC POLITICS

As already mentioned, regional resistance to the civil rights movement occurred most prominently and commonly through Democratic Party dominance of Southern politics. White Southerners routinely conducted their grassroots politicking, selected their political leaders, and charted their public governance within the Democratic Party and its primary, which was then tantamount to official election. Southern Democracy, exercised in accord with historical and regional custom, thus was a semi-legal way to continue white rule despite the civil rights revolution.

There was little nuance in the belly of the Southern political beast at the beginning of this period. Real politics and race-gaming was a simple case of stubborn resistance, physical intimidation, and continued segregation. While demonstrations, laws, rulings, and troops forced certain institutional adjustments, Southern politicians adopted informal but intense and effective tactics for continuing the Southern way of life.

Three general malpractices—partisan race-warring, white-black manipulation, and biracial corruption—exemplify the continuing, cynical strain of Old South racism.

DEMOCRATIC RACE-WARRING

In the most blatant version of traditional race-gaming, Democratic white politicians commonly and successfully ran racist campaigns and conducted racist governance throughout the South. This abuse of responsible democracy worked because racist candidates enjoyed strong support in the polarized environment of majority white one-partyism. As the civil rights movement progressed, these race-wars constituted a struggle for the soul of old-style Southern Democracy as much as campaigning for public office.

Alabama presented a classic case of the power and influence of race in the 1960s. By 1966, thanks to the Voting Rights Act, approximately 200,000 new black voters had joined the half-million white voters in the Democratic primary. When elected in 1962, George Wallace was constitutionally limited to a single term; so—fresh on the heels of promising "segregation forever," standing in the schoolhouse door, and winning several Democratic presidential primaries—he ran his wife, Lurleen, in the 1966 Democratic primary for governor. Nine men (including two former governors, a former congressman, and a sitting attorney general) also lined up for the top job and future direction of the Heart of Dixie.

Lurleen Wallace's official theme was her husband's slogan, "Stand Up For Alabama," and George generally preached regional populism—or what Dan Carter called the "politics of rage"—on the campaign trail with her.[47] But the real story of that election was racial politics in Alabama and the South. As Montgomery civil rights activist Virginia Durr wrote to a friend, "'Stand up for Alabama' does not mean one damn, single thing except to prevent integration."[48]

Two especially brave challengers—Alabama Attorney General Richmond

Flowers and former U.S. Congressman Carl Elliott—attempted to end the Wallace Era with a coalition of moderate whites and newly enfranchised blacks. Elliott was the favorite of the national party establishment, while Flowers hoped to ride a large black following to success in the primary.

Flowers openly sought the black vote by talking about civil rights:[49]

> When I'd speak to black groups I'd tell them, "When I'm governor and you come to Montgomery, you're gonna get jobs, and I don't mean with mops and brooms. You're gonna get good jobs behind desks and typewriters. Not because you're black. You won't get a job in my administration simply because you're black, but you'll never be turned down for a job just because you're black." That was what they wanted to hear, and they'd all cheer and shout.[50]

Flowers was cited by the *New York Times* as "the first major white candidate in modern times to campaign directly among Negroes in the Deep South"; he was endorsed by the Alabama Democratic Conference and most other black political organizations. Later analysis indicated that he got nine of every ten black votes in the primary.[51]

While Flowers concentrated on black votes, Elliott attempted a biracial campaign.

> Meanwhile I went about courting blacks and whites alike, refusing to go to either extreme for the votes of one of the other. I summarized my stance in a speech in Selma: "I have not come to Selma tonight to stand on the Edmund Pettus Bridge and shout *'Never!'* Nor have I come to stand in the Brown's Chapel AME Church and sing 'We Shall Overcome.' There must be a middle ground for Alabamians."

Elliott's pitch for black votes was, in his opinion, honest and straightforward.

> I didn't cozy up to them, I didn't back away either. When I made a speech in the town square in a place called Greenville, three times as many

black people were in the crowd as white. When my talk was done, I shook hands with the crowd, black and white alike. Then I went inside to pay my respects to the probate judge, who hadn't come out to hear my speech. I began to thank him for the privilege of speaking at his courthouse when he suddenly cut me off.

"You," he said, as if pronouncing judgment from the bench, "have violated Southern tradition, shaking hands with those niggers."

As I was walking away, this judge came out and hollered right there in front of the crowd, "You've gone around and shaken hands with these *niggers!* No white man's ever done that around here before."

I turned and said, "Well, this is a new kind of day, and I'm a new kind of white man."[52]

Elliott's politics played well in sympathetic circles—he eventually was honored as the first recipient of the John F. Kennedy Profile in Courage award in 1990. However, in Alabama of the 1960s, he scored little respect among either white or black voters.

Mrs. Wallace won the nomination with more votes (54 percent) than all her male opponents combined; Flowers was a distant second (18 percent), and Elliott placed third (8 percent) in the record primary turnout.[53] The Democratic nominee then went on to trounce Republican Jim Martin, by a better than 2–1 margin, in the general election.

Flowers himself has acknowledged his miscalculation of the Alabama political situation during that period:

> That was my biggest disappointment in politics. When I ran for governor, I was thoroughly confident. My polls had told me, with the black vote I was going to receive, I could win with a small percent of the whites. That's one time I was completely wrong. I took a calculated risk and lost. I thought I had it figured, but I didn't. . . . I guess I should have kept talking about the Southern Way of Life.[54]

Elliott, a respected, moderate congressman of that time, likewise described his quixotic adventure in biracial politics as an ill-fated experience: "That campaign turned pretty ugly fast." He said "a bunch of hooligans physically pushed us off a stage" in Bessemer. The Klan tore down his signs. There were bomb threats. His workers were run off the road. Some were shot at.[55]

Both Elliott and Flowers were eliminated as significant, moderating voices in Alabama politics. And more bad news was to follow in their personal lives. The former congressman struggled with painful memories of his biracial efforts and severe financial hardships at the end of a celebrated career. The former state attorney general would soon face federal extortion charges (for which he would be found guilty, eventually was paroled, and finally was pardoned by President Jimmy Carter).

More significantly, that 1966 election turned George Wallace from a one-term segregationist governor into a long-term national phenomenon. It also set Alabama on a course of race-warring for years after the civil rights movement, during which time New South Democrats were unable to crack Wallaceism in this little corner of the world. State Senator Ryan deGraffenreid (who had lost to George Wallace in a 1962 Democratic Party primary runoff) died in a tragic plane crash mid-campaign against Lurleen Wallace in that 1966 primary. Albert Brewer (the lieutenant governor who had moved up temporarily to the governor's office upon Lurleen's death from cancer in 1968) came close, but his chance perished at the hands of George Wallace and vicious racism in the 1970 primary. Lieutenant Governor George McMillan fell victim to a strange twist of racial politics in the 1982 primary when some blacks supported George Wallace's last gubernatorial campaign. Without serious Republican opposition in the general election, these critical, internecine party primaries generally stalled biracial progressivism.

As a political science professor at Jacksonville State University in the 1970s, I studied the public record and electoral statistics of those early exercises in race-marred democracy; I also did a lot of polling on Alabama politics as a consultant. While outright race-warring of the above sort tapered off as a general practice, I observed the ominous power of race to contaminate both sides of the racial divide; this single factor had the awesome potential to disrupt virtually every aspect of Southern public life.

I discovered that sometimes, in some locales, under certain conditions, there was no market for open, bold, biracial leadership. My research as a consulting pollster in one community showed that whites and blacks were so polarized that my candidate's only course to victory was pure race-gaming. Separating personal inclination from client obligation, I candidly assessed his electoral option: "Realistically, you're not going to get any black votes; so you may as well try to energize and maximize your white base."

The intensity and immensity of the race problem convinced me that there would be no easy, consensual, conclusive solution to the Southern racial dilemma; I would have to exercise extreme caution and commitment if I were ever going to contribute constructively as a leader in Alabama politics and American democracy.

WHITE-BLACK MANIPULATION

As an integral part of generalized race-warring, the traditional game of whites-manipulating-blacks within the façade of democratic governance has long been a matter of common knowledge. Political scientists easily and often documented this practice during the post-movement period of Southern history.

Donald R. Matthews and James W. Prothro, for example, observed in *Negroes and the New Southern Politics* (1966) that many white politicians did not know what to do about the newly registered voters, but they began to adjust, in limited and indirect manner, to changing ways:[56]

> As our informant put it, "They obviously can't go out hell-bent seeking colored votes." Nonetheless, they have made some covert appeals—the road supervisors have graveled some driveways, and roads that had been neglected for years have been repaired. Perhaps the day has come when such officials can no longer say they do not "give a damn about a nigger road."[57]

Of course, this progression of biracial politics did not move Southern society very far along the road to equality.

> Where whites are so fearful and hostile toward Negroes that politi-

cians run the risk of losing two white votes for every Negro vote gained, candidates are not likely to be overtly responsive to Negro wants and needs. Where the white vote is less predictably and less overwhelmingly anti-Negro, some ambitious politicians will try to build a biracial coalition of supporters. Even when this strategy works . . . the Negroes in the coalition are likely to receive a smaller "payoff" than their numbers merit. And such a coalition is very fragile—the white segment of the coalition may desert the first time someone cries "nigger." Because the Negroes can rarely win without white allies, especially in races in large geographical districts, they have to settle for considerably less than half a loaf or give up eating bread altogether.[58]

Additionally, numerous studies depicted standard practices of racist manipulation as the heroic drama impacted traditional Southern politics. A team of political scientists from the University of Florida—Alfred B. Clubok, John M. De Grove, and Charles D. Farris—conducted field research explaining with specificity how Southern white politicians routinely manipulated black voters to exercise the closed politics of white rule.[59] They depicted racial relationships in which black registration and voting were encouraged, facilitated, and organized by and for the benefit of the white political structure. The electoral activists—both white and black—were primarily the agents of members of the white political structure; and the preponderance of blacks simply voted in response to the activists as agents of the whites.

"Organization and manipulation of a Negro vote," they wrote, "was conceived of as a means of either obtaining or retaining control of public policy-making positions." They described the process in one community thusly:

> In Hamlin the city judge and sheriff, along with the police chief who is recognized as a subordinate of the sheriff, handle the actual organization of the Negro vote. Before an election barbecues are held for the Negro voters on the ranch of the city judge. Negroes are driven to the ranch in trucks, and barbecue, fish, liquor, and beer are apparently in plentiful

supply at this type of election meeting. On the day of the election the organization swings into high gear. A hired crew of Negro "street walkers" canvasses in the Negro community as agents for the whites. The street walkers are provided with a list of registered Negro voters, and it is their job to produce the voters at the polls. The street walker is usually provided with money, some of which may be passed on to voters, but it was our impression that the money was used to defray the cost of mobilizing the vote and, of course, for the street walker's own commission.[60]

In other communities, the researchers found similar activities and techniques. There were barbecues and fish fries, church meetings, and, of course, substantial sums of money. "Apparently some of the money makes its way to the voter—there appears to be a semi-professional group of vote-sellers in the town, both Negro and white—but most of what is spent is used to defray the cost of mobilizing the vote."[61]

Fortunately, legal prosecutions and changing public probity increasingly discouraged such racial manipulations, at least as large-scale operations, in the Southern political marketplace.

BIRACIAL CORRUPTION

While early race-gaming normally involved flagrant racial wars with white manipulation of vulnerable blacks, some interesting patterns of biracial corruption—with predictably un-civic ramifications—developed among white politicians and black activists in the post-civil rights movement era.

As the heroic drama faded, Southern elections turned into more highly developed enterprises, and questionable players, practices, and motives crept into the still relatively closed but burgeoning business of black electioneering. Increasingly, white campaigns exploited black electorates; black operatives exploited white campaigns; and, in the process, white and black players mutually abused the democratic process.

Public officials, academicians, and journalists have generally avoided this aspect of Southern politics. It does not reflect well on leaders of that era, either white or black, to talk about the "buying" and "selling" of votes in the extended shadows of heroic drama; most current scholars seem uncomfortable probing such historic matters because of the hypersensitive racial angle; and even media types have not been very interested in digging for information about the twisted racial practices of Southern elections during that period.

However, Larry J. Sabato and Glenn R. Simpson cracked the code of silence about race and money in Southern elections in *Dirty Little Secrets: The Persistence of Corruption in American Politics* (1996).[62] While their book was broadly focused and bipartisan in its criticism (based on interviews with hundreds of politicians and operatives), they scored a remarkable breakthrough in a short section on loose cash and minority votes in Southern campaigns. In a few pages, they drew a stark picture of relatively unseen, unchecked, illicit abuse in the peculiar politics of Southern Democracy.

Here's how the system worked in a typical Southern campaign, as explained by Sabato and Simpson:

> In the black community, ministers, officeholders, and "voter league" leaders are critical to Democratic organizing efforts, and they are explicitly targeted. But the means necessary to secure their endorsements and cooperation vary from the wholly legitimate (pledges by the candidate to back certain policies and programs) to the seedy (transfers of large amounts of money to key individuals). In return, black ministers typically endorse their chosen candidates from the pulpit on the Sunday prior to election day, and they provide church membership lists to campaigns. Minority officeholders can lend their political operatives and personal networks of backers. And black voter leagues each distribute their trademark "sample ballots" at the polls, with their chosen candidates highlighted.[63]

On election day, the campaign shifted to turnout:

> Even in a less ambitious effort, hundreds of flushers are hired: they are frequently black high school students organized by a Democratic teacher, or college students who have the scheduling flexibility to spend all of Election Day prowling minority neighborhoods for potential voters. The flushing activity becomes frenzied late in the day as poll closing time

approaches. . . . Each flusher is typically paid $20 to $50. Fleets of cars, buses, and other vehicles are also at the ready to ferry voters to and from the polls, with the drivers paid expenses plus the flusher's fee. For every two dozen flushers or drivers there is a coordinating supervisor, paid up to $100 for the day's work. Supervisors are often loyal party workers, but the cooperating ministers and community leaders normally get to designate a fair share of these vote captains. Some are also checking the rolls at the polls, to see which predesignated black voters have not yet cast a ballot and need to be found and transported.[64]

Sabato and Simpson raised concerns about both electoral and moral excesses in these operations:

As we have fully acknowledged, some aspects of street money are completely legitimate, including small election day payments to flushers and drivers and phoners. And many, probably most, minority political activists and ministers are well-motivated, hard-working individuals who participate in party politics because they believe in it. But few will even try to justify some of the outrageous practices we identified earlier in this volume: large unaccountable "tribute" payments to some black ministers, the gravy train for certain minority entrepreneurs, the political money shell game that defeats the purposes of disclosure laws, the offering of near-bribes such as free gasoline as an inducement to vote, and so forth . . . Whatever the truth of that, it seems rudely ironic for a community that shed much blood to secure a right so wrongly denied its members for centuries to now acquiesce in the selling or renting of that right—or even callously treat it as a mere business proposition.[65]

My analysis thus far conforms to the conventional version of Southern politics. Southern Democracy politicos—mainly white and some black—practiced a politics that reflected continuing racism in post-movement years. That would change.

THE DECLINE OF TRADITIONAL RACE-GAMING

Fortunately, the South lurched forward and real Southern politics began evolving in a different manner in the 1970s. Traditional racial campaigning and manipulation declined; legal scrutiny discouraged corruption; and public opinion constrained other unsavory practices. Most certainly, moreover, the surge of black voters into the Democratic Party and the shifting of white voters to the Republican Party impacted traditional politics. The old regime of massive, conservative, white, one-party rule began to lose fashion and functionality.

Interestingly, too—either as part of the cause or as part of the conse-quence—a new breed of white officials and black activists entered the picture at this stage. Some leaders—mainly Democrats—played a positive role in the region's transition from loud, raucous, racist one-party dominance to a more moderate politics and real two-party competition.

It was not easy, of course. These new-breed politicians had to figure out, during this volatile period, how to represent a changing society—that is, courting and serving blacks without being punished by the white majority. In effect, many successful politicians had to assume semi-phantom roles and conduct partially underground operations during the days of Southern Democracy. They played a different version of the race game—obviously with mixed motives—during these critical and evolutionary times.

As explained in the next section, these white politicians and their black allies helped moderate the shameful ways of real Southern politics, and the race game evolved systemically during the 1970s, '80s, and '90s.

While my account portrays a continuum of cynical racial practices throughout much of Southern history, there is an intriguing subplot of hushed positive and progressive endeavor in the post-movement period. In this section, I want to talk about a new kind of leader and a different kind of politics.

NEW LEADERS AND NEW-STYLE POLITICS

A significant key to Southern change from the 1970s through the 1990s was the quiet, practical, biracial politics practiced by many Southern white public officials and black activist allies.[66]

These leaders purposely and positively addressed black issues, without unduly antagonizing the white majority, while pursuing normal missions and careers as Southern public officials. They and their activist allies worked independently at various levels and areas throughout Southern Democracy; they helped change the nature, rules, players, issues, and outcomes of the Southern race game. They quietly and practically incorporated black and white voters, activists, and organizations into their election campaigns, and they worked, together, to articulate moderate policies and provide more equitable public services to both black and white constituencies. At first slowly and cautiously, with measured success, then increasingly as the situation allowed, they helped move things forward without the attention and trauma of the preceding two decades.

I should interject, as a point of editorial clarification, that this new style of leadership is simply a variation of my analytic focus on the "race game" and "real Southern politics." The important and pertinent fact is that Southern Democracy was altered, to a significant degree, through the relatively progressive but quiet, somewhat secretive, sometimes uncomfortable, oftentimes less-than-noble, biracial service of practical white politicians and black activists during the closing decades of the twentieth century.

I know about this new-style politics because I was one of these new-style politicians. As I have explained elsewhere:

> I got into politics because I was concerned about American democracy. I knew that, in order to pursue my personal democratic interests, I had to be an effective, responsive, and responsible public official in terms of broad concerns of importance to my base white constituency and to those of the black minority. So, over the course of my career, I publicly concentrated on political reform, fiscal responsibility, and national security issues. At the same time, I diligently but less-publicly focused on race and racism. I worked very hard and quietly to secure enough black support to get elected in majority white areas; I sincerely tried to be fair, moderate, and progressive in my politics; and I didn't talk much publicly about any of this stuff.[67]

More direct are the remarks of Dr. Joe L. Reed, one of the most important black leaders in Alabama during the past half-century:[68]

> Throughout history, and especially in the days following the civil rights movement, we worked quietly with white friends. That quiet politics of accommodation was the only way we could accomplish anything during those times. You sure couldn't go to the top of the mountain and tell everything you knew and what you were doing with white politicians. There were some of them that we wanted to give awards to but we never could because it would have killed them if it got out about what they were doing for blacks.

ALABAMA TRAILBLAZERS IN THE NEW POLITICKING

Southern Democracy had passed its peak by the time I entered the political arena, and I cannot claim to have blazed the trail of new politics.

I include within the trailblazing category Alabamians like Bill Baxley (who was one of the first successful white politicians to openly solicit black votes and support black causes); Don Siegelman (whose career provides critical insights about pursuing progressive, biracial objectives amidst powerful, antagonistic interests and constituencies); and John Teague (my early political mentor who showed me how to mix biracial progress with the raw politics of Goat Hill).

However, my ultimate model of quiet, practical, biracial leadership during that era was the late Howell Heflin, who traveled a progressive course as chief justice of the Alabama Supreme Court (1971–77) and U.S. senator (1979–97).

In many ways, Heflin represented the prevailing traditions and culture of Alabama, but on some issues he went against the grain in his Deep South state. A Southern Democrat, he was pro-defense, supported the right to bear arms, and opposed legal abortion; he also supported school prayers and opposed gay rights. Economically, he sometimes sided with the anti-tax Republicans and at other times he went with populist Democrats. And, much to the consternation of conservative elements, he generally supported civil rights and affirmative action.[69]

On the other side of the relationship were black leaders who just as cautiously—for obvious reasons—dealt with white politicians. In Alabama, for example, civil rights icons like Joe Reed, Richard Arrington, Fred Gray, and numerous others often worked quietly and practically with the Heflins, Baxleys, Siegelmans, and Teagues to win elections and push relatively progressive causes.

These trail-blazers might quibble with my characterization of their leadership; however, all of these political leaders (and numerous others not cited here) contributed in important ways to quiet, practical, biracial reconstruction in Alabama. While I never replicated exactly their particular practices or achievements, I derived guidance from their collective experiences and employed those lessons in my own career as a politician.

My Experience in Changing Racial Politics

In the following pages, I will try to give the reader an insider's version of the changing racial environment during those days. First, I will discuss various aspects of racial politicking in Montgomery and Washington; then I will share my experiences as a politician in the evolving race game.

Special Challenge and Unique Opportunity

As I've mentioned elsewhere, relatively few political scientists (actually relatively few political leaders) have ever experienced such challenge and opportunity as I have enjoyed in politics. I have had a long, rewarding career as professor-politician, studying and teaching American democracy and government in South Carolina, Georgia, Alabama, California, and all over the world. But my most effective and memorable educational experiences took form and place in the historic environs of Goat Hill (as the state capitol complex is known) in Montgomery, Alabama. Most pertinently, I worked—in a legislature struggling in both figuratively and literally cramped quarters—to overcome our hard history; my future work as secretary of state and congressman simply extended that experience to broader issues. In a relatively short period of time, I was fortunate to be present and active in the development of a working relationship between Alabama's legacy white power structure and heroic black leadership, two groups of people who just a few years previously had engaged in dramatic confrontations that captured national and world attention. In truth, I would have paid to participate in those historic times and virtual seminars on Goat Hill.

As an Alabama legislator during the 1980s, I served in the very chamber where Alabama seceded from the Union, where Southern delegates created the Confederate States of America, and where the Confederacy was head-quartered for a while in the 1860s. As Alabama secretary of state, I often walked out of my office and paused in awesome reflection, outside the front door of the Capitol, where Jefferson Davis was sworn into office as president of the Confederacy, where George Wallace issued his "segregation forever" speech, and where the Selma-to-Montgomery march terminated.

I worked with some of the heroic and villainous characters of the civil rights movement—although most had already gone on to other lives or places for their respective rewards or punishments by the time I arrived on the scene.

I helped Governor Wallace on reform issues during his last term, getting to know him as a person and politician (he eventually cut a rare commercial endorsing me when I ran for Congress). George Wallace had stood in the schoolhouse door but later confessed his sins, asked, and received forgive-ness from Alabama's black citizens.

I associated with the likes of Fred Gray (who had served as legal counsel for Dr. King, Mrs. Parks, and countless other civil rights cases), Dr. Joe Reed (longtime civil rights activist and head of the Alabama Democratic Confer-ence), and Dr. Richard Arrington (mayor of Birmingham and founder of the Jefferson County Citizens Coalition). As lawyer and legislator, Fred Gray did more than any single individual to bring down segregation in Alabama; Reed and Arrington were preeminent in transitioning Alabama politics from white massive resistance to biracial practicality. All three helped substantially in my campaigns and career.

RACE AND POLITICS IN THE HEART OF DIXIE

It did not take me long to form some generalizations about my white and black associates, our dilemmatic relationship, and my course in the post-civil rights era. In the following discussion, I'll describe and comment on changing racial politics and relations, focusing first on my white colleagues.

White Leaders

To begin, I would say that most white leaders during that time knew that a new day had dawned in their state; they did not like it, but they accepted the reality of a new, biracial politics. While everybody understood that racism and racist politics would continue into the future (not simply by purposeful action but because of the difficulty of quick fixes for historical dilemmas), most whites realized that there had to be significant accommodation in Alabama and Washington, whether through changing attitudes, affirmative actions, or even simply institutionalizing biracial racism.

Developing bifactionalism—a struggle between relatively liberal groups and relatively conservative opponents—provided the essential political framework for policy/issue/governance during my tenure in the Alabama legislature (1982–86). There was no real two-party system at that time, and thus the formal legislative leadership—handpicked by Governor Wallace and dependent upon an alliance of education, labor, black, and trial-lawyer interests known as "the Democratic Coalition"—structured the process to enact moderate/progressive legislation against loosely aligned forces of conservative Democrats and an increasing number of Republicans. I usually sided in these disputes with the Coalition. This course was in keeping with my politics; it helped develop essential relationships; and it proved useful when I started pushing my own reform agenda.

The Democratic white leadership in particular embraced the new way of doing business. They figured that compliance—bringing blacks into the process and sharing power and policy—was the only way to continue their control of the process, especially in light of a growing Republican presence. These practical white leaders, in concert with the coalition of special interest groups, thus changed the system, incrementally and pragmatically, to establish internal power-sharing arrangements with black politicians. Of course, some Democratic white politicians never accepted or changed; they continued to rant and obstruct. Some switched parties. Many inevitably faded from the scene.

BLACK LEADERS

When I began working with and forming extensive relationships with African Americans in Montgomery and throughout the state, I concluded that—other than obvious historical differences and public posturing—most black leaders in Alabama were like white leaders in Alabama in that they were politicians eager to assert their new influence on important public policy. They were no more nor less noble and no more nor less political than their traditional adversaries. For the most part, they were interested in the same things as white politicians—improving the state's education system, economic development, jobs, and social services, while also looking out for black constituencies, other disadvantaged people, some powerful special interests, local areas, and pet causes. At the same time, they were just as inclined as white politicians toward personal power, patronage, and perks.

In terms of political and socioeconomic backgrounds, black leadership in Alabama was expanding during those years. While the civil rights movement was still a potent rallying cry, and while most black leaders in the state still derived their electoral support from the combined base of religious and civil rights organizations of the 1950s–'60s, the elected officials in Montgomery and even in the local areas increasingly were more secular, independent, and professional as politicians. Educators and lawyers prevailed among their ranks rather than the ministers and activists of the old days.

It surprised me somewhat that black politicians were not generally fond of civic legislation such as education, election, and constitutional reform. I had figured that they would be natural allies in these efforts; in reality, they were not very interested in these matters of great concern to some of us white leaders and the outside media/civic community. I attribute this disinterest to two related historical developments. First was the fact, stated earlier, that Southern white society had long suppressed and ignored what went on in black society as long as it did not disturb or egregiously offend the white world. Therefore, white politicians managed and manipulated the black community for whatever gain was there, and certain practices and ways developed among blacks beyond the scrutiny of broader government and society. Secondly, I concluded that since my black colleagues had gained power and services through the rules of the political game played in that shadowy arena, they were not keen on changing those rules, even for progressive reasons. Quite often and understandably, for example, they viewed ideas like increasing school standards and cleaning up voter lists as contrary to their interests and those of their black constituents. So I usually had to sell—not always successfully—my reform initiatives to them as both progressive leaders and vested politicians.

PARTY POLITICS

The Alabama legislature was undergoing partisan change in addition to racial accommodation during that era. Republicans were of mixed politics and sentiments. Politically, the Republicans (all white, of course) had different ideas of what the state legislature was about: they prioritized limited government, low taxes, a favorable business climate, and pro-family/morality issues. Especially in the beginning, the Republicans had fewer outright racists in their ranks; the old-line business types dutifully accepted change and biracial politics in principle. But, besides natural partisan debates about the government's role in dealing with racial, social, and economic problems, some of the political practices of the new day offended them—and they vociferously attacked the Democrats for race-based political dealing. Also, the insurgent Republicans relentlessly assailed ethical shortcomings of the Democratic establishment. As a civic democrat, I agreed with the Republicans on numerous matters regarding legislative procedures and various reform matters. But I was a Democratic Party team player, with responsibility for governing rather than posturing, and I stuck with my team. Later defections of disgruntled conservative Democrats regimented and standardized racial, political, and philosophical divisions between the Democratic establishment and the growing Republican caucus.

RACIAL POLITICS

Even as the civil rights struggle stretched into its fourth decade, old ways did not yield easily on Goat Hill. Race served as a common, everyday prism for business in the legislature, and black-white differences served as the flashpoint for daily argument among competing factions. All of us knew that the small band of black legislators (variously numbering about 15–20 of

105 members in the House and about 5–6 of 35 in the Senate) comprised a loyal, determined, disproportionately powerful part of the Democratic Coalition. They were interested in every issue; they were ready to fight at any moment; and they demanded satisfaction—or there would be hell to pay. For example, there usually were other, very important items on the day's schedule that depended upon their procedural cooperation simply for deliberation; besides, any black complaints were taken very seriously then by the U.S. Justice Department.

Consequently, the public debate often degenerated into shouting matches about fairness, justice, racism, and corruption; none of us was ennobled in the process. Sometimes, the House leadership proceeded without the black legislators, and occasionally it ran over them; but most major policy victories included an accommodation to key black leaders who were vital to the coalition's broader agenda of issues and governance.

Beginning with the organizational session, for example, the leadership coordinated with key black legislators regarding committee assignments and policy agendas; daily voting schedules were negotiated on racial grounds. Thereafter, virtually all matters involved black-white haggling, whether the issue was state budgeting for education (which required special appropriations for traditionally black schools), appointments to state boards/agencies/commissions (which had to be racially balanced), state government contracts (which required minority set-asides), state employment practices (which required equitable hiring goals), state employee pay raises (which had to be weighted toward lower-level workers), state tax policy (which had to consider business-class-race disputes), and law enforcement and criminal penalties (which were almost impossible to legislate due to emotional and disparate impacts).

Reapportionment (redistricting of electoral boundaries) was a special nightmare of monumental racial ramifications. Even congratulatory resolutions were scrutinized to make sure they were sensitively worded and without hidden agendas. Inevitably, anything that might benefit one side or the other in a two-sided argument relating in any way to black-versus-white—past, present, or future—was a racial crisis.

This problem was especially frustrating for those of us interested in fundamentally reforming the Alabama political system. We found that it was virtually impossible to address obvious and serious problems—whether it was education reform, election reform, constitutional reform, tax reform, welfare reform, anything involving systemic progress—without running into racial obstacles among both white and black legislators; each side was unwilling to consider change because it might hurt them in the historical struggle of white-versus-black.

Such problems, of course, were simply part of that era in Alabama politics. Effective reconstruction posed continuous challenges to practical, biracial leadership.

THE BROWDER AGENDA

I pursued a good-government political career in Montgomery, voting moderately/progressively on issues of the Democratic Coalition, staying out of frequent frays between racial hotheads, and maintaining good personal relations with individual black legislators and organizations. I carefully articulated explanations for some of my relatively liberal actions for the broad white populace, and I discussed more delicate racial matters in private, quiet sessions with black politicians. This may sound rather simplistic, but in the polarized environment of the 1980s, that was quite an assignment.

In pushing education improvements, for example, we encountered significant black opposition to the Education Reform Act which I was sponsoring for the administration. Many blacks opposed it as a threat to black interests. However, we neutralized some of that opposition by incorporating black organizations and leaders in the process; we reminded them that, as part of the package, I was sponsoring a 15 percent across-the-board pay raise for public school teachers, perhaps their staunchest financial supporters and campaign workers. Some of my black colleagues also balked when I introduced a new program that automatically fined lawbreakers to help reimburse victims of violent crime; they argued that it was going to hurt their constituents disproportionately since blacks were quite often hauled before the courts of justice. They backed off when I showed them evidence that most victims of violent crime were African Americans, who suffered severe financial hardship because of those crimes (I also assured them that

Governor Wallace would name a black to the three-person governing board of the Victims Compensation Commission).

Things weren't always that easy or successful. It was almost impossible, for example, to get biracial support for my election reform initiatives such as campaign finance disclosure, cleaning up voter lists, and combating absentee ballot abuse. It was no secret that campaign operatives worked relatively free of public, media, or legal scrutiny in certain parts of the state; while I could usually round up significant white support, there didn't seem to be any sentiment among black officials for changing that situation.

Sometimes, furthermore, our biracial endeavors exploded into nasty public incidents and headlines. For example, in my first year in the legislature the federal courts ordered us to redistrict legislative boundaries to make the system more racially reflective of the Alabama electorate—and that meant dumping some whites for blacks in a quick special election. I helped the Democratic Coalition shift the party nomination from a few of my conservative white colleagues to favored black candidates, a blatant, brutal move on our part. I bled emotionally and politically for my part in the notorious "hand-picking" scandal, but it significantly expanded African American representation in the Alabama legislature.

To repeat, I rubbed shoulders with a few genuine civil rights "heroes"— black and white—in those days of change, and I worked with many practical veterans of the previous era to move things forward and constructively. However, I learned first-hand that crass racial politicking was a bipartisan and biracial phenomenon in Alabama. This did not surprise me—after all, politics is politics; also, I knew it was a well-deserved nuisance tax from aforementioned legacies and I simply lived with it. But it was a real part of Goat Hill politics—and added to the challenge of my practical assignment— during that period.

POLITICS AND RACE IN THE NATIONAL CAPITAL

Later on, I pursued my public career as U.S. congressman from east-central Alabama. My academic and political background in Alabama prepared me well for service in the U.S. House of Representatives.

As expected, there were major differences between Alabama and Washington, and I would have to deal with some tricky angles immediately upon moving from Goat Hill to Capitol Hill.

The issues in Washington were more comprehensive and consequential—the American economy, national security, and international relations. The personalities and egos were bigger—President Bush, President Clinton, Speaker Wright, Speaker Foley, Speaker Gingrich, Majority Leader Gephardt, Majority Leader Armey, and various icons who went simply by the title of "Mr. Chairman." And the constituent pressures were greater—fighting the federal government for people back home, telling the local community that their military installation might close, and raising large sums of campaign money.

Most importantly, I found that civic and racial challenges in Washington were formidable. I settled into the congressional system as a moderate, centrist politician—with good government and reform inclinations—and I worked in a bipartisan way during my tenure in Washington. I usually sided with the Democrats; however, I discovered that, just as in Alabama, the Democratic establishment was not very enthusiastic about my good-government or reform agenda. Throughout my congressional service, therefore, I struggled to organize and promote civic issues unpopular with my party.

In Alabama, I had been a key player on the relatively progressive team that ran the show. Even as a member of the majority faction—which included both whites and blacks—it had been very difficult to push and implement good-government initiatives. In Washington, I took a seat as an "outlier" in the neverland of Southern white Democrats who often found ourselves in the crossfire between our own party and the opposition Republicans; the GOP takeover in 1995 pushed me further to the sidelines. Throughout, I constantly jockeyed among various organizations and issues of black-white consequence at home. Under those circumstances, my prospects for meaningful reform were virtually nonexistent.

A CONTINUING RACE GAME

It was also clear to me that race and racism were alive and well—although more subtle and sophisticated—in the national capital. Earlier, while discussing Alabama politics, I acknowledged the constant, dominating, routinized role of racial considerations in the changing Heart of Dixie. Actually, however, white leaders in Alabama often pursued progressive government in private concert with black leaders, a candid, cooperative, personalized relationship that was facilitated by our shared legacy of hard history. But race relations in Washington were distant and strained.

I found the course of biracial politics in the United States Congress to be more public and showy—but also more impersonal and cynical. Both Democrats and Republicans, white and black alike, professed color-blind and civil rights principles; but pertinent transactions often resembled the same insider game of crass, race-based wheeling-and-dealing for public acclaim and special-interest power. Maybe I looked at all of this through the eyes of a white Southern sentimentalist, but sometimes racial politics in our national capital seemed just a refined rendition of what happened back in Alabama.

Interestingly, as suggested in previous paragraphs, I found it more difficult to pursue quiet, practical, biracial leadership in Washington than back in Montgomery. As a Southern white politician in D.C., I carried history and stigma amid alien pressures that made my job much more burdensome.

Most white Southern politicians—particularly Democrats—who seriously wanted to provide positive biracial leadership and enjoy career political success during those times knew that an essential part of successful politics was an objective, instrumental, coldly calculating regard for race, racism, and constant scrutiny. All the while, as we vigilantly avoided and opposed racist politics, we knew it was there in the heart of a significant portion of our people, both white and black.

Clearly, my career changed when I went to Congress, and I left Washington with mixed feelings. While I thoroughly enjoyed the bigger challenges and greater responsibilities, congressional politics drew me deeper into things like staff meetings, committee hearings, and just keeping the federal government going. And raising campaign money—which I hated. Serving in the Alabama House had been fun; serving in the U.S. Congress was work. It was rewarding; but it was hard going and long hours. My one term in the state legislature had been a productive calling, an enjoyable time spent in the company of friends and fellow legislators at an important point in a changing race game. In Washington, I could go for days in the bureaucratic maze without seeing any of the Alabama delegation.

I also found that national service drew me further from my reform and good-government mission. Washington is a high-pressure operation of old-style politics, and I didn't get very far with my brand of good government. It also bothered me that I had to deal with the old race dilemma so carefully and testily in a congressional body that had racial problems of its own. I found it very difficult to "do good" and conduct quiet, practical, biracial politics at the national level of American democracy.

So let's talk more specifically about what I consider my contribution to quiet, practical, biracial transformation of Southern Democracy.

ADVENTURES IN QUIET, PRACTICAL, BIRACIAL LEADERSHIP

My role as a new-style leader of that era is the subject of another book, so I'll not go into full detail here. However, I would like to share a few insights and comments about those times.

To generalize, the challenges, realizations, and realities of black-white politics in Montgomery and Washington were valuable aspects of my practical education; they simultaneously facilitated and complicated my participation in the race game and real Southern politics.

For the record, throughout my career, I represented fairly typical Southern constituencies that were about three-fourths white and one-fourth black. I was generally known as a civic-minded public official with a moderate record and responsive support for African American issues.

A SPECIAL GAME PLAN

I never articulated an official, public strategy for quiet, practical biracial politics—but I tried to provide disciplined leadership for good government and racial progress in hard-historied Southern politics. I actually developed a discreet, personal game plan for pursuing biracial politics and my own agenda of civic reform and good government.

My campaigns, for example, were designed and conducted to secure significant black support without driving away the white majority. I kept black campaign activities low-key and sometimes separate from regular campaign operations. I consciously avoided situations in which the opposition might depict me as the "black candidate." I made sure that there were mixed faces at my events in the black community; and I didn't spend a lot of time at all-black public meetings, arranging instead for brief drop-ins or stand-in representatives. I tried to minimize the racial orientation of my black media advertisements, and those ads usually ran in select areas late in the campaign.

In translating these campaigns into actual governance, I had to take my game plan to a higher level, adjusting my leadership style—and improving my skills—as I experienced success and setbacks in my racial endeavors.

I learned to build quiet coalitional power—including black and white participation—for my agenda of civic reform and racial progress. These latter two elements were inextricably linked in my version of Southern progress; considering regional history, I felt that the race factor needed to be positively spun, neutralized, or at least minimized in public discussion.

To get anything done of a civic or reform nature, we had to have significant black support or at least black acquiescence, and to do anything in the nature of racial progress, we had to have significant cooperation from whites. The truth was that, given Alabama's past problems and contemporary demographics, a few noisy white reactionaries or a few black rabble-rousers could mess up everything for the rest of us. I may have overestimated the problem in some situations, but I knew from my academic background, consulting experience, and political practice that the opposition would do anything to thwart civic and racial progress. Therefore, I incorporated my particular approach to politics—adjusted for the situation at hand—pretty regularly in those days.

I simply avoided talking about racial issues or tactics because anything I said would have been used against me by white and black opponents. I never raised certain topics and I dismissed probing from the opposition and media people by shifting the conversation to a broader discussion of real and important concern. For example, when pushed on something like the Confederate flag question, I would brush it off with a comment that "I don't want to get into that kind of talk" or "That flag controversy is just something to divide us and keep us from dealing with problems like social security and education." When quizzed about racial aspects of voting or crime, I would talk about reforming election laws and drug laws to protect democracy and society at large. When asked point-blank about the role of blacks in my campaign strategy or political administration, I would proclaim "I want to represent everybody!"

MODERATE SERVICE

Analysis of voting data in the Alabama House and the U.S. House documents that I practiced moderate politics and sometimes support for minority causes over the years. In Montgomery, I was a solid pro-education vote (95 percent), and I supported the business line much less often (38 percent). In Washington, I established a balance among education interests (64 percent), the business community (63 percent), and organized labor (65 percent). On ideological rankings, I normally scored at about the midpoint between the most conservative and most liberal members of Congress (54 percent conservative and 46 percent liberal, according to National Journal data covering social, economic, and international affairs). I supported Republican President George H. W. Bush 46 percent of the time and fellow Democratic President Bill Clinton on 66 percent of recorded votes.[70]

Amid this balanced moderation, I was selectively attentive to the agenda being pushed by African American organizations. No quantitative assessments exist for my service in the Alabama legislature or as secretary of state, but in Congress I registered slightly above the average member—53 percent—on civil rights issues during my career (as reported by the Leadership Conference on Civil Rights, a broad coalition of black and other human rights groups). I considered this mark impressive for a liberal scorecard that counted such items as a balanced budget amendment and campaign finance disclosure as anti-civil rights legislation. By comparison, my Democratic predecessor compiled an LCCR career rating of 24 percent and my two Republican successors have scored even lower ratings (12 percent and 17 percent).

I never cast a "yea" or "nay" for racist reasons or racially blinded my conscience, but I tried to be politically prudent, balancing my racial record just as I did on education, business, and labor issues. I continuously looked for opportunities to promote racial fairness and justice; however, sometimes

I took contrary positions, despite how any special interest group might score that vote.

In the Alabama House, for example, I loyally supported appropriations for black colleges and universities; I voted for legislation promoting the appointment of black deputy registrars; and I supported reapportionment plans for increasing black representation. But I abstained from voting on the Martin Luther King Holiday. In the U.S. Congress, I voted for reauthorization of the Civil Rights Commission, for the Hate Crimes Statistics Act, for Historically Black Colleges and Universities, and for several extensions of the Civil Rights Act. On the other hand, I opposed the use of statistical race-disparities as a defense in death penalty cases and I supported limitation on race-bias claims in death row appeals.

In fact, during my congressional career, I voted for a full two-thirds of real racial issues on the LCCR scorecard (when the list was purged of such nonracial votes as the balanced budget amendment, campaign/lobby reform, health/welfare proposals, business-labor provisions, gender matters, gun control, and immigration).

I think the record will show also that I practiced fair, biracial politics in terms of staff employment, constituency service, and special initiatives on behalf of my constituents.

Impact?

Overall, I enjoyed many successful campaigns and my years in public service. I like to think that I provided quiet, practical, biracial leadership and that I contributed to a new and different Southern politics.

I must also admit that my circumspect approach to racial politics probably helped terminate my public career. The truth is that this style of politics was a transitional phenomenon. We helped reconstruct traditional ways; but our kind was destined to fade away as a new era of racial customs and partisan politics swept through the South.

I'll not elaborate further in this manuscript. But readers may ask, legitimately, whether there was a real and broader "movement" of service and reconstruction as has been described in this chapter. So I will cite the results of a survey of some of my former Southern congressional colleagues about their quiet, practical, biracial service during this evolving period of Southern politics.

THE BROADER SCOPE OF QUIET, PRACTICAL, BIRACIAL PROGRESS

As part of a related research project, Dr. Artemesia Stanberry (a political science professor at North Carolina Central University) and I surveyed a handful of former members of Congress from Southern districts to determine their representational styles in terms of the thesis of quiet transformation. All eleven of the white ex-politicians quoted in this manuscript had represented majority white districts with significant black constituencies; they had compiled voting records of 50 percent or better on civil rights issues. They looked like a good group to probe, and the results of our survey were rich and positive.[71]

Judging from the survey, numerous public officials throughout the South were attempting this new and different kind of politics during the 1970s, '80s, and '90s.

Their representational styles varied. However, most of our surveyed leaders reported that they conducted important activities—administered either within or separately from their formal campaign or service institutions—targeted specifically for the black community. The significant finding is an extensive agenda of relatively progressive activities rather than the exploitative ways of the traditional Southern race game.

Most importantly, at least at the beginning of a campaign, they aggressively solicited the personal allegiance of influential individuals in the black community, including church ministers, public officials, civil rights activists, the media, various professionals, and friends. Ronnie Shows (Mississippi) offered an example that communicates the special importance of person-to-person politics in campaigning for the support of a key black activist in one of his early races for the state legislature:

> I waited most of the day outside her house until she came home. I asked her if my opponent ever came to her house, and she said he sent somebody. I asked her if he ever put up signs or handed out campaign cards in her community, and she said no. Then I told her that she and her

people were voting for an official who was supposed to represent everybody and he didn't have enough respect to come and ask for their support. She didn't say anything, but she asked me for my pencil and wrote my name on her ballot. I won that runoff by a thousand votes, and that lady's granddaughter was my first page as a Mississippi state senator.

CONSTRUCTIVE PUBLIC SERVICE

All our respondents reported that these campaign activities easily continued into their service as public officials. They hired black staffers and served black constituents; they opened the political process and governmental offices to the black community; and they addressed issues of concern to black citizens through their votes and in other ways. Representative Martin Lancaster of North Carolina probably spoke for numerous white Southern colleagues in saying that the manner in which he represented the people without regard to race set a positive tone for the district:

> My representation of all segments of my constituency was as fair to every segment as I could possibly be. I sought out the views of leaders in the minority and was receptive to contacts made by the minority community . . . In whatever endeavor I was ever involved in (from the Red Cross to the County Library Board) I always advocated for proportional representation of the black community on the boards and in leadership positions.

Tim Valentine (North Carolina) felt that white Southern politicians had to prove themselves to their black constituents; so he made it his business to convince them that he could and would represent blacks:

> I hired black staffers in my district and Washington offices. I was seen in the black community. I was available. We were dead serious about constituent services. We answered our mail. My door was open to all whom I represented. I supported all civil rights legislation . . . In short, I tried to conduct myself so that African Americans would have to understand that we intended to treat them with dignity and fairness.

Other members seemed to serve their black constituents with an individualized style that emphasized impartial service and minimized race-conscious operations. According to Roy Rowland (Georgia):

> I hadn't really thought about it, but I guess my relationship with the black community was about the same as it was during my time in medical practice . . . As a physician, I had contacts with many blacks on a very personal basis, I always treated everybody with the same respect and care. That was true in my public service as well.

Likewise, Bill Alexander (Arkansas) said:

> My family taught me to be friends with black people . . . Just treat people fairly and don't make a big deal out of it.

Owen Pickett (Virginia) provided a particularly striking account of personal service to his minority constituency.

> Black leaders mainly wanted access and an open line of communication to make sure their views were heard and fairly considered. I have had black ministers call me in Washington and request that I join them in prayer on the telephone when an issue of particular interest to them was coming up for a vote.

My overall conclusion is that all of these leaders figured out—whether purposively or not, separately or not, happily or not—how to successfully court and serve their black electorate without arousing undue ire from their white majority. The next section suggests specifically and generally their reconstructive imprint on Southern politics.

POLITICAL PROGRESS

It is evident that our surveyed leaders took pride in their contributions to the changing politics of that era. Whether talking about their "firsts" on behalf of blacks, their stands on controversial issues, or their patterned fairness in representation, the respondents considered themselves positive biracial leaders in an uneasy time for both blacks and whites.

Robin Tallon (South Carolina) stressed bold initiatives during his career in politics:

> The black community was always a priority for my office. As an example, in my first term in office, I successfully lobbied our senior U.S. Senator, Strom Thurmond, chairman of the Senate Judiciary Committee, to support and report out of the Judiciary Committee the Martin Luther King holiday legislation . . . Also, I came out publicly for removing the Confederate flag from the state capitol. I felt that if a significant percentage of the population was offended, then it made sense to remove it and get on with other issues that affect everyone's everyday life.

Pete Peterson (Florida) articulated a mindset that probably was pretty common among Southern white politicians during the latter years of that era:

> I was always keenly aware of my obligation to represent the interests of my constituents—particularly my black constituents for I felt that they had historically been unrepresented in the district. As a result, almost as an auto response, I would find myself evaluating legislation, government agency activities, environmental decisions and other government actions for their potential impact on the black communities or black people in general. Legislative issues associated with civil rights, agriculture, environment, transportation, jobs, housing, and education were the prime areas of concern among my black constituents and I worked to improve legislation wherever possible to ensure that black communities got their fair share and a fair shake.

Virginian L. F. Payne, who seemed unsure about how to classify himself in terms of our thesis, was definitely positive about his biracial mission and record:

I told my constituents that my job was to represent all citizens and consider all points of view; and we had a total open door policy, which wasn't the case in the past. I tried to let the black community especially know they were being heard and represented.

Georgian Lindsay Thomas was also ambivalent about the thesis, but he acknowledged a strategy of racial cooperation and measured progress rather than one of confrontation.

I represented a traditional Democratic district with adequate moderate support in the white community that never put me on the cutting edge on racial matters. Quite frankly, I never had to worry about these matters with the support base that we had. Certainly there were extremists who would have polarized the communities had they had the chance, but they simply never gained the traction that the responsible leaders in both communities had and maintained. I guess I was just lucky. . . . However you call my style, I would say that it allowed a constructive environment in which we could concentrate on the issues that affected everyone's daily lives.

SYSTEMIC CHANGE

Generally speaking, my former colleagues seemed to understand and cherish their roles in changing the fundamental nature and course of Southern history.

Perhaps this sentiment was best expressed by Butler Derrick (South Carolina). Drawing from his broad perspective as a proud citizen and long-time public official in the state that fired the opening shot of the Civil War, he philosophically mused about Southern absolution:

I like to think that I was doing what was best for the country . . . that I was helping to remove the 'mill stone' of segregation and inequality that had hung around the neck of the South for so many decades . . . I think we made the African American community feel more a part of the process;

and we helped make the white community understand that they had a common interest and benefit in progressive government.

When all was said and done retrospectively, this simple survey conveyed a picture of varying service styles among selected politicians of that time in this region. Despite mixed reactions to my particular conception of their leadership, these former members of Congress attested to the reconstructive nature, activities, and accomplishments of quiet, practical, biracial leadership throughout the South.

AFRICAN AMERICAN AFFIRMATION

Obviously, such talk from white politicians has to be subjected to some validation—so I asked a few black leaders of that period to respond to my ideas about changing Southern politics and to tell us about their reconstructive dealings with white officials back then.

I earlier cited the comments by Dr. Joe Reed affirming the practice and progress of such politics ("That quiet politics of accommodation was the only way we could accomplish anything during those times."). Equally corroborative are the words of Dr. Richard Arrington Jr., who along with Reed has played a dominant role in Alabama racial history of the past half-century:[72]

> I agree that quiet, effective, biracial cooperation was a cornerstone of much of the heralded and hard-won racial transitions in Southern attitudes and politics. Without it, the courageous and well-recorded acts of the modern civil rights movement would have had a much more difficult course; in fact, my own political participation was grounded in such politics as much as in the movement. I can think of numerous important people—white and black working together—who quietly laid foundations for my career and changes in our area. I doubt that they knew at the time just how productive and far-reaching their actions were for biracial progress in the South.

Jerome Gray will suffice as "Exhibit A" specifically evidencing this assessment. Gray, longtime field director for the Alabama Democratic Conference, recently recounted several cases of progress during this period in Alabama:

> In the 1970s, ADC asked and got commitments from candidates Jimmy Carter, Howell Heflin, and Donald Stewart that if they got elected they would support the appointment of black federal judges in Alabama. The evidence shows that they cooperated and kept their word to the black community.
>
> We collaborated with black State Representative Fred Horn and white State Senator John Teague in 1983 to pass legislation virtually requiring the appointment of black deputy voter registrars in Alabama. Although the bill was essentially about bringing uniformity to the voter reidentification and purge process, we used this opportunity, through our friendly collaborators, to include a landmark provision in this bill that said that "boards of registrars shall appoint one or more deputy registrars in each precinct in the county for a four-year term, running concurrently with members of board of registrars."
>
> We achieved considerable success during the 1980s and 1990s in getting many majority white governmental entities throughout the state to voluntarily change historically discriminatory systems for electing local leadership. Through quiet and practical negotiations, we succeeded in convincing a number of officials to cooperate in these changes.[73]

Without doubt, the most compelling witness to the concept is storied civil rights attorney Fred Gray of Tuskegee, Alabama. Fred Gray's role in the civil rights movement stretches beyond Alabama, to broader Southern politics, and even to the core of American democracy. He represented Mrs. Rosa Parks in integrating Montgomery city buses; he was the first civil rights lawyer for Dr. Martin Luther King Jr.; he litigated representational discrimination through *Gomillion v. Lightfoot*; he successful challenged Alabama Governors John Patterson and George Wallace and various state agencies on important civil rights issues; he fought the United States government for justice in the Tuskegee Syphilis Study; he was one of the first African

American legislators in Alabama since Reconstruction; and he was the moving force in establishing the Tuskegee Human and Civil Rights Multicultural Center. A mild-talking but determined civil rights champion who is still active, Gray adds unimpeachable testimony to the thesis:[74]

> Yes, the thesis is valid and any research that can be presented will do a good service for our understanding of Southern politics and history. The civil rights movement began long before the 1950s and extended beyond the 1960s; and a lot of people don't realize that it took many forms—not just big legal cases and dramatic protests against segregated buses, schools, and facilities. Most white politicians and black leaders didn't even talk to each other during the 1970s, so those of us who could work together did some things quietly and in back rooms. I fought in the courts for most of my life, but a lot of good things happened, legislatively and otherwise, through this kind of politicking among practical politicians.

These observations from former members of Congress and African American leaders confirm the reality and impact of quiet, practical, biracial reconstruction during that period.

THE DEMISE OF SOUTHERN DEMOCRACY

Ironically, racial progress of the past several decades wrought inevitable demise of both quiet leadership and traditional politics in the South. The new-style leaders were transformational but transient; in a way, they may have fallen victims of their own success in helping change Southern Democracy.

In the beginning, during the 1970s, these politicians had proceeded quietly and practically within the traditional regime. The key challenge back then was how to deal tactically and tactfully with the mainstream conservative constituency of white voters in the Democratic Party primary; coalitional blacks were just coming of age in the normal political process, and Republicans were no more than a vocal nuisance. Then, in the 1980s, it became possible to pursue moderate politics more aggressively and successfully. However, these positive developments simultaneously sowed the seeds of decline for such leadership in the 1990s. As time passed, the large, conservative, white constituency began splitting off and casting its votes elsewhere; blacks became more politically mature, independent, and assertive; and Republicans became more powerful in exposing and defeating these leaders in the general election. Certainly, too, enhanced media coverage and advances in campaigning injected powerful new elements of transparency and volatility into the process, making quiet, practical, biracial maneuvering less feasible and effective.

The shift from old-style Southern politics to new-style Southern politics undermined the fundamental nature and asset of quiet, practical, biracial leadership. Such politics was essentially over, though unremarked, toward the end of the century.

Nevertheless, the collective consequence of these efforts represents an important evolution of Southern politics that supplemented the civil rights revolution. Unnoticed at the time, and viewed askance today, these efforts may seem meager by comparison to the heroic drama. Arguably, however, these white and black leaders accomplished Southern change in a way and to an extent that was beyond the reach of federal officials, laws, and troops. And while righteous souls and racial ogres dominate the pages of history books, these reconstructionists helped bring black voters into Southern elections, helped end racist control of the Southern political establishment, helped moderate Southern governance, and, in a roundabout way, helped nudge the South from Southern Democracy toward real two-partyism and a new order of politics.

Our analysis in this chapter has noted several transitions in Southern politics and the race game over the past half-century—from the Old South, through the civil rights revolution, through massive resistance, through quiet transformation, through black empowerment, through the growth of two-party competition, and on toward the end of the twentieth century.

Now things are changing again, dramatically, in the twenty-first century. Of course, most scholarly and media attention these days focuses on Southern partisan developments, particularly GOP reddening of the Deep South. However, just as consequential in terms of the region's racial future is a contemporary phenomenon that defies easy assessment. In a way, the current situation is simply an extension of real Southern politicking to a more openly progressive stage of biracial interaction, so we might view modern white-black relations as just a more publicly practiced version of the historic race game. But closer examination shows that this is a distinct, qualitative evolution of that game; the South has now strangely embraced and accommodated historical and political realities.

In the next chapter, I will elaborate the new order because it is indeed a systemic evolution in the race game of Southern history.

IV

A New Racial System for the Twenty-First Century

I MAGINE ROSA PARKS FINALLY agreeing to ride in the back of the bus, now
equipped with Lazy-Boy recliners across that back row. Imagine Bull Connor serving Southern sweet iced tea to demonstrators as they stroll amiably
along the sidewalks of Birmingham. Picture the Bloody Sunday marchers
being shuttled respectfully from Selma to Montgomery by Alabama State
Troopers in air-conditioned squad cars, lights ablazing and sirens ablaring.
Or, can you envision George Wallace cheering Tuskegee and Alabama State
at the annual Turkey Day Football Classic and Martin Luther King tossing
the ceremonial coin for the Auburn-Alabama Iron Bowl a couple days later?
All of these "imagines" occur, of course, under the vigilant and approving
guidance of the Civil Rights Division of the U.S. Justice Department.

Such conjured scenarios are weird exaggerations. But they serve to emphasize a striking evolution in the race game and real Southern politics. A
"New Racial System" prevails in the twenty-first century.

Of course, there's not much public talk among the politicians themselves
about a new system of race relations, especially if the conversation smacks
of race-mongering or unprincipled racial compromise. Southern officials
have to be wary in their comments, lest they offend mainstream society or
run afoul of their own racial constituencies. So, even while pursuing positive
change, they tend to respect the norms and traditions of the divided cultures,
negotiating contentious problems on an ad hoc basis, sometimes openly and
sometimes privately, and in a way that allows personal political flexibility

or, if necessary, tactical resort to the old ways of Southern history.

I am no longer a practicing participant in contemporary Southern politics, and surveying current officials about this phenomenon would probably prove academically useless. But I am sufficiently wired into the regional system through focused observation and informal conversation with friends and associates to have a continuing, solid basis for my assessment of the new racial relationships.

The academic community and professional media have yet to focus on this aspect of black-white relations; obviously, there's no proclaimed code of procedures for such politicking. Therefore, it is difficult to articulate— clearly, concisely, and authoritatively—the changed role of race in real Southern politics.[75]

So, what is going on in the South?

In this section, I will present my thesis of the South's new racial order, and I will explain the new system as a sophisticated yet awkward and sometimes unsavory—but generally biracial and functional—accommodation of regional change among both Southern politicians and the Southern people.

THE NEW SYSTEM: A HALFWAY HOUSE OF RACIALIZED POLITICS

A half-century after the civil rights movement, blacks and whites in Alabama and the South seemingly have come to terms—terms that will amaze outsiders—about living together in a halfway house of racialized politics. A New Racial System has taken hold as the region develops a biracial, functioning politics despite its hard racial history.

For most Southerners, the Old South is dead; Southern Democracy is a memory; the Republican Revolution has been consolidated; and two-party competition is a reality in various parts of the region. Most importantly, descendants of slaves and slave-owners have reconciled pressures for systemic progress with certain aspects of their cultural pasts; and the civil rights movement of the 1950s–'60s has morphed, rather curiously, into a new order for the new century.

My original statement of the Southern race game has changed substantially and significantly during the period of our interest. As a reminder, that traditional system was designed to provide whites with the blessings of democracy while oppressing, exploiting, and discriminating against their fellow human beings of African origins and heritage. The new order is a more conventional operation, without base objectives of racial oppression, exploitation, or discrimination. Clearly the game favors white majorities and their conservative priorities, but black minorities now participate and their concerns often take center stage.

Today's major controversies therefore are not matters of slavery, segregation, or anything near civil rights crises of the past. Of course, critical fights still occur over rancorous racial policies and practices; debate rages over issues related to racial history and class distinctions in this part of the country. Normally, blacks demand bold government initiatives and whites insist on less bold action as a result of these debates and fights. However, the new game revolves mainly around disputes about more routine decisions of policy and politics—or "who gets what"—with, expectedly, whites and blacks on different sides of partisan struggles.

This is neither the stark past nor an idealized future; it is a halfway house of racialized politics in which white politicians and black politicians attempt to secure for themselves and their constituents the blessings of democracy and the goodies of political life. Furthermore, as the rest of this chapter will illustrate, both sides now exhibit an appreciation of a new racial culture and a working relationship of biracial accommodation in pursuit of these blessings and goodies.

Neo-Racial Culture

As Southern Democracy receded and Republicanism spread, a neo-racial culture of Southern politics—absent universal, egregious, consuming racism but "still revolving," as Key might say, "around the position of the Negro"—took root in the 1990s. This new racial outlook thrives as we begin the twenty-first century.

Apparently, participants in the Southern political system have come to accept the idea that (a) race and racism are real, critical, unavoidable legacies in the public arena, and that (b) moderated race-gaming is an appropriate way to do political business in contemporary regional democracy.

A perfect storm of changing contextual forces—demographics, economics, black votes, partisan realignment, moderating attitudes, and constant legal pressures—has brought many Southern white and black politicians together in an incongruous arrangement on important issues and day-to-day workings of Southern politics. Almost incredibly, this togetherness reflects their raw history and current relationship. They used to engage in brutal race wars in which white leaders oppressed, exploited, and discriminated against blacks; but now, even though they often divide and dispute racially, white and black politicians more often than not negotiate racial transactions for mutual benefit and/or progress. In fact, successful Southern politicians on both sides play this race game—even if they don't like the game or each other.

The logic of this approach is straightforward in a society which has shed sinister racist ways yet where race constantly—consciously and subconsciously—colors public life. Many political clashes involve real partisan/philosophical/ideological differences; and the outcome is more likely to reflect conservative priorities rather than the liberal agenda. However, practical Southern politicians, activists, voters, and journalists have adopted this neo-racial mindset to deal directly and functionally with the South's historical dilemma. This mindset injects racial considerations into discussions about most general operations of Southern government, including taxing, budgeting, hiring, and oversight; and it intrudes especially into sensitive negotiations on such diverse matters as education, law enforcement, public employee pay raises, and even campaign reform. Inevitably, the new racial politics impacts—sometimes constructively, sometimes shamefully, sometimes shamelessly—the way we conduct political and public business in the contemporary South. Unlike in the Old South and Southern Democracy, however, these racialized transactions are conducted within the framework of "moderated race-gaming"; contemporary white-black politicking usually produces workable outcomes and sometimes encourages progressive action.

In essence, then, the new arrangement is a continuing game of racial politics—now played by both whites and blacks in more sophisticated manner without traditional perversities—in a regional system still struggling with historic black-white tensions. This new order represents a modern-ized, measured mixture of hard history, progressive practicality, and, most importantly, biracial accommodation.

Biracial Accommodation

As has already been stated, the new order essentially is a case of white and black cooperation in peculiarly regional fashion. Peaceful coexistence— Southern style!

Modern Southern politics is indeed biracial in the sense that constitutional white supremacy and statutory segregation have yielded to openness and opportunity for blacks to participate. But the South's implementation of "biracialism" could just as well be labeled "bi-racialism"—with a hyphenated emphasis on racial divisions of power, race-sensitive deliberations of policy, and sometimes dualistic programs for whites and blacks. Furthermore, "bi-racialism" often smells of "bi-racism" as politicians pursue electoral arrangements and governing outcomes for their own racial interests and to placate their racial constituencies. Both white and black politicians seem super-sensitive to the still competing cultures in this troubled land.

Interestingly and importantly, white Southern politicos have been joined by many blacks, liberal interests, and governmental agencies in adopting this approach because it serves select purposes of progress and practicality. Race-based policies and practices have now become routine options in regional politics.

There's a lot to be criticized about the halfway house of racialized politics, but it has proven functional and stable in this region. Biracial accommodation has survived—very alive if not well—the lingering stench of racism, civil rights litigation, judicial scrutiny, fiscal concerns, and begrudged acceptance among blacks and whites.

It is not pretty civics; it's just the continuing legacy and evolving politics of hard history. Race is the acknowledged, powerful continuity in a new game whereby both whites and blacks now biracially accommodate important adjustments and routine politics in regional life. The practice of racial politics varies from state to state and even within states, and much remains to be improved. But I believe that my analytical construct accurately depicts and explains real change throughout the Old Confederacy.

Thus this is a qualitatively different racial system featuring new cultural ideas and approaches to politics. As demonstrated in the rest of this chapter, the new regime can be distinguished from that of yesteryear in substance, style, strategy, operations, and outcomes.

SUBSTANCE

Simply and centrally, contemporary Southern politics is more moderate in its issues and more progressive in its practices than what happened in the Old South or the post-civil rights movement South during the latter decades of the twentieth century.

Numerous factors—such as demographic adjustments, cultural shifts, legal pressures, partisan developments, and moderating politicians—figure into this regional progress, but a key explanation is that African Americans have joined the political process as competitive and cooperative agents of change. As a consequence, outright racism is no longer a common staple of electoral campaigns, and state and local governments now pursue more equitable priorities.

The South is still a conservative region; the racial divide continues to impact the political process; and biracial accommodation among politicians has yet to translate into full fairness and equality in broader Southern society. But the New Racial System is substantively different from Southern politics of the past.

STYLE

In terms of style, the new politics is more open and honest about race, in mainly positive ways, than were previous politicians.

As previously mentioned, Southern society has shed sinister racist ways of the past, but race constantly, consciously, and subconsciously impacts public life. Sophisticated Southerners recognize the reality of their racial legacy; they have adopted more genteel, yet direct, manners in conducting the political business of contemporary regional democracy.

Hence the changing public face and discourse of the new Southern politics. Race continues as the most useful, single factor of both analysis and power in the South, but people down here understand that they have to adjust their language and conduct to political realities and a new way of life.

Consequently, the tone of Southern politics has softened and racial issues have blurred into broader, more substantive, and conventional considerations among the diversifying Southern populace.

STRATEGY

The new politics also involves strategic considerations reflecting the end of massive, white, conservative, one-party rule with rigid systemic constrictions on African American participation. Coalitional thinking—involving blacks in a serious manner—now predominates in Southern politics.

In most parts of the modern South, political strategy incorporates the possibility of biracial political success and even black self-determination—in a variety of cultural environments, majority-minority settings, amid real Democratic-Republican competition. Even when outright victory is impossible, biracial coalitions and minorities usually parlay their agendas into the wheeling-and-dealing of Southern politics. And, as already noted, the new racial strategizing is mostly straightforward and out in the open.

It seems, for example, that in every election in the South, there's articulated hope for a controlling, moderate, color-blind and bipartisan center of political strength; but, in most instances, this strategy confronts the reality of race-tinged politics in a reddening constituency, especially in the Deep South. Then the fight usually turns into Republicans (mainly white) against Democrats (disproportionately black). Sometimes, whites and blacks ally in successful, competitive endeavors—that is, behind some candidates, in some years, in some races, and in some policy initiatives—particularly in the Peripheral South.

Furthermore, in some locales with African American majorities—such as Birmingham, Atlanta, and other big cities and in certain parts of the Black Belt—blacks exercise electoral and governing power, befitting their numerical dominance, for minority and progressive causes.

Race thus continues as an underlying factor, but it is now strategically employed—acceptably, by whites and blacks alike, by Democrats and Republicans alike—for real political and philosophical gain wherever and however, as contextual situations demand and/or allow in the new order.

That's not radical, avant-garde politics, but it's different from the old days of one-party rule throughout the region.

Operations

Operationally, regional politics has changed considerably with the coming of a new order and convergence between the South and America; in many ways, activities in this region are amazingly similar to what would be considered normal party politics in other regions.

Southern politicians, political parties, and organized interests now run common, almost cookie-cutter electoral campaigns; and, as noted, whites generally ally with the Republican Party and blacks solidly back the Democratic Party. Both parties possess ample resources, powerful technologies, and precise practices that empower them to aggressively target, energize, and serve their base constituencies.

In terms of governance, the contemporary situation resembles a kaleidoscope of operational contexts. The practice of biracial politicking normally prevails in Democratic Party circles (obviously less so among Republicans), in areas where black-white issues are prominent, throughout the South. Most commonly, and necessarily, policy-making where the two races share power resembles a dual system of governance in which dominant leaders and factions of blacks and whites compete and then consensually check-off on any final program of consequence (ironically, somewhat like the process of concurrent majorities envisioned by John C. Calhoun). This makes for tough going at times; but it's the only way to get anything done considering Southern racial history, constant legal oversight, and the contemporary political environment.

It is clear that race still plays into political operations, but not as fractiously as before; many Southern officials and citizens—both white and black—now function in working alliances and normal operations along ostensible lines of conventional issues.

Outcomes?

Summarily, Southern politics has evolved toward a somewhat normalized system—mainly conservative of course—in which black-white politics plays a central role. Most players—the politicos and the public—seem to understand, shrug, and accept the game and its outcomes.

But is this new order fair? Or is it just a cosmetic makeover for old-style politics and race-gaming? Does this arrangement reflect political progress in terms of policy and programmatic outcomes for black Southerners? Is it a positive sign for the future of the Southern political system? These questions are legitimate, and the answers are hedged in the analogy of the half-empty, half-full glass of water.

Case Study of Accommodated Progress

Perhaps the best way to convey and illustrate the South's sense of accommodated progress is to examine the formal court decree—in *Knight v. Alabama* (2006)—addressing historical racial discrimination in Alabama's higher education system.

Alabama, like many Southern states, has settled with African American litigants through an extensive action plan; it is attempting to correct its discriminatory past by pursuing a variety of commitments to "prepare all its students for productive lives in the twenty-first century."[76] The agreement—signed by black plaintiffs and the public universities and accepted by the federal courts—entails significant efforts to eliminate vestiges of de jure racism in funding, faculty, staff, student recruitment, and other programs through remedial endeavors.

While *Knight v. Alabama* (2006) targeted discriminatory vestiges at mainly white universities such as Alabama and Auburn, the outcome actually solidified a dualistic system of black and white higher education. Left legally intact was a network of traditionally black schools such as Alabama State University, which was created in 1867 as the state's minority teachers' college.

In the final judgment, African American plaintiffs endorsed the state's good faith efforts; and the court effectively announced full compliance with the law:

> By entering into this Agreement, the Plaintiffs acknowledge that the defendant University has satisfied this legal burden to warrant termination

of this Decree with respect to defendant University. The parties agree that good faith efforts to enhance diversity should continue, and that continued progress does not depend on continued federal court supervision. The defendant University pledges to continue to make good faith efforts to further the progress that has been achieved over the course of this litigation in redressing historical discrimination in higher education against African-American citizens of this state, and reaffirms its good faith commitment to operate in a constitutional and non-discriminatory fashion.[77]

Furthermore, neither side seemed interested in pressing the matter any further, agreeing that:

> ... there are no continuing policies or practices of defendant University, or remnants, traceable to de jure segregation, with present discriminatory effects which can be eliminated, altered or replaced with educational sound, feasible and practical alternative or remedial measures.[78]

The important outcome, of course, is that Alabama higher education is now striving for openness and diversity; much progress has been made in remedial funding for minority programs and black institutions.

But at the same time Alabama continues to accommodate, in effect, predominantly white colleges and predominantly black schools. In a state that is about three-fourths white and one-fourth black, the major public institutions are disproportionately one way or the other. Today, for example, the University of Alabama is about 80 percent white and Auburn University is about 90 percent white; Alabama State University and Alabama A&M University have similarly high percentages of black students—both in the 90 percent range—on their campuses. And there are few complaints.

The current situation seems to be a mutual compromise for achieving racial progress while accommodating traditional institutions, preferences, and ways of the black and white communities. The parties involved have struck an anachronistic bargain incorporating "freedom of choice" into an education system previously separate and now trying to be fair and equal— from a distinctly regional, historical, and cultural perspective.

Some look at such developments and shake their heads. James Hood, who integrated the University of Alabama with Vivian Malone Jones in the 1960s, expressed disappointment upon returning to the campus for the fortieth anniversary of that event and seeing students of different races eating in different areas of a campus cafeteria:

> I realized that segregation was still there, but now it was self-imposed— and I wondered what the struggle was all about. Looking fifty years after *Brown* we have to ask, have we done all that we can do to further our objective, and have we made a demand that there be an inclusive agenda? And the answer to both is no.[79]

But many—including the federal judiciary, black leaders, and several other Southern states—consider such arrangements as acceptable progress, or at least realistic necessity, in this region. Courts have declared similar settlements in Louisiana (1994), Tennessee (2001), and Mississippi (2004). This year in Georgia, a proposal for combining a few black and white institutions, for fiscal reasons, received little support. Erroll Davis, chancellor of the Georgia University System and an African American, implied the realities in saying that "I don't think economics will drive the decision; it's going to be a political decision." Black State Senator Vincent Fort said the proposal will get a stiff fight from the alumni of historically minority institutions: "The associations for these black schools are very protective of their legacy." Former Fulton County Commission Chairman Michael Lomax, who is now president of the United Negro College Fund, dismissed the idea as neither a "thoughtful or timely suggestion."[80]

Thus a new version of race relations—as elaborated in this discussion of substance, style, strategy, operations, and outcomes—seems to have taken hold in Southern political life. Admittedly, not all Southern public officials practice the politics described in this manuscript. Some—particularly conservatives—are disinclined toward "progressive" endeavors; others— whether by principle or personality—simply refuse to play the game of racial politics. And in some areas, it's not necessary or possible to practice such biracial accommodation.

Call it what you may—terms like "peaceful coexistence" and "racial feudalism" readily come to mind—the South now practices a new political order reflecting its history of bilateral cultures and collateral institutions. There's a commonality of region and governance; but increasingly Southern politics is conforming to the broader context of Southern society, as evidenced in patterns of housing, schools, sports, and religion. I suspect that most contemporary Southern politicians pursue conventional objectives and racial progress, in measured, practical manner, while striving to preserve certain valued aspects of their past and present. This is a functional adjustment of the Southern way of life, without perverse contortions of the past.

In the following section, I will discuss a recent academic portrayal of the new way of doing political business; then I will present some of my own observations from inside the current race game of Southern politics.

AN ACADEMIC PORTRAYAL OF THE NEW RHETORIC OF RACE

Political scientist Matthew J. Streb introduced the altered nature of contemporary racial politics in *The New Electoral Politics of Race* (2002), in which he observed that race—or at least the rhetorical version of racial conflict—is an increasingly missing issue in American democracy.[81] More pertinently, he posed a central theoretical and practical question about racial politics in the South:

> Almost forty years after Wallace's inaugural pledge, the politics of race has changed dramatically. De jure segregation is no longer legal and tensions between blacks and whites have diminished. The influx of large numbers of African Americans into the electorate has forced politicians, especially Democrats, to court black voters. Racial rhetoric like that of Wallace's 1962 campaign, which at one time carried candidates to victory, now causes candidates to be labeled as "extremists." So what happened? How did America's major "dilemma" just disappear? Or has it?[82]

Streb sought to resolve what he termed "the race puzzle" by examining racial strategies in seven gubernatorial elections of the 1990s (Alabama, Arkansas, Georgia, Iowa, Massachusetts, Ohio, and Virginia).

Content analysis of campaigns in these states led Streb to conclude that public debate has indeed moved beyond the racial rhetoric of the civil rights movement—but race remains at the heart of both Southern politics and American democracy:

> It's not that race is now unimportant, it's just that the way we talk about the subject has changed. In many ways, campaign strategies appear to be color-blind without really being color-blind . . . Instead of petitioning black voters through explicit racial issues, candidates now use implicit or non-racial issues to attempt to win African American votes. On the surface, candidates' platforms may seem color-blind, but it would be wrong to conclude that they no longer see distinctions between blacks and whites (or other groups for that matter).[83]

Streb explained, furthermore, that the key to electoral success was developing a campaign style that turned the public debate from civil rights to other issues—such as the economy and cultural matters—in still-racially sensitive environments. Successful candidates in his studies strategically sought to position themselves on selected issues—mainly through implicitly racial or nonracial politicking—to maximize their chances of compiling biracial majority support.[84]

Additionally, Streb found that regional and partisan considerations figured into those strategies, but not exactly like before. While race remained prominently on the Southern agenda because of the demographics and history in that part of the country, he noted little difference in racial rhetoric between the Southern and non-Southern campaigns. He also found that both Democrats and Republicans incorporated implicit racial pitches into their delicate calculations.

Streb reported too that the competing parties addressed and responded to black interests in appropriate settings:

> If racial issues are not discussed anymore, does that mean that African Americans are not being represented? Not necessarily. As the case studies illustrate, Democrats are reaching out to African Americans through issues

such as health care, job creation, and education . . . Even Republicans, as the Arkansas and Virginia case studies show, can reach out to black Americans through issues of morality and religion.[85]

Streb's research clearly showed the changing nature of race relations in the South.

AN INSIDE REPORT ON THE NEW POLITICS OF RACE

I can confirm—drawing on my background inside Southern politics—both positive and negative aspects of the New Racial System in contemporary electioneering and governing.

In this evolving system, new-order Southerners candidly calculate and calibrate racial factors—while carefully avoiding divisive rhetoric and moral stigma—in their particular spheres of regional politics. Most commonly, competing politicians and parties try to appeal to both sides of the ideological spectrum in moderate public discourse. Seldom is heard the language of "white supremacy" and "black separatism"; but critical operations are geared to their respective hard-core constituencies. Behind the scenes and through functionaries, white and black Democrats and Republicans play to their core racial bases with battle-tested calculations and calibrations of issues and resources.

Illustrative is the now standard and demanding formula for successful election in Southern politics. Few promote it enthusiastically in public discussion; however, Southern political insiders—politicians and operatives, whites and blacks, D's and R's alike—understand, and they've conducted formulaic racial campaigns for the past quarter century.

In Alabama, for example, culture, demographics, and history dictate, in shorthand politicalese, that a Democrat usually needs to win 90 percent of the black vote and at least 40 percent of the white vote to get elected to public office statewide; but a Republican can win with 60 percent of the white vote and only 10 percent of the black vote. Obviously, the numbers vary and shift according to the particular candidates, issues, and venues, but this statistical framework is the initial fundament of Alabama politics. Most successful Alabama politicos automatically think in such terms, and they develop and implement specific percentage targets for their political endeavors. While most campaigns pitch a moderate, positive, nonracial theme, the tactical priority for both Democrats and Republicans in this process is how to energize their racial bases; when elections get tight, their immediate inclination is simply adjusting their campaigns appropriately for greater base proportions and turnout without violating moral standards and legal constrictions.

Quite often, such campaign practices work in acceptable manner and direction. Sometimes, however, as politicking intensifies, the race game retrogresses; and in difficult contextual situations, leaders of both races and parties demean themselves and the democratic process on behalf of loud constituencies, narrow objectives, and backward politics. These politicos incorporate powerful new technologies and resources into semi-segregated operations, thereby exaggerating racial considerations in a political system that still suffers from racist history. Often, when push comes to shove, Democratic candidates just recalibrate their racial calculation, rhetoric, and finances to hustle total black allegiance; Republicans run coded ads to gin up their white constituency to maximum levels of emotional and electoral support. It's not a very inspiring approach, and it sometimes leads to patently racial electioneering.

This approach also dominates post-election dealings behind closed doors—in Montgomery and Washington. Public debate normally involves grand ideas about fairness, openness, and opportunity for the middle class and working people; but in the closed confines of political power the discussion is clear and direct, spoken in the language of specific policies and other payoffs according to racial considerations. Particularly on the Democratic side of the partisan aisle, white and black leaders negotiate, often cordially but sometimes heatedly, on important considerations of politics and policy. Critical issue positions, legislative votes, employment practices, political appointments, redistricting efforts, constituent services, financial arrangements, and other aspects of prospective public service have been subject to race-gaming for several decades. (I've never been in Republican back rooms, but such considerations similarly involve core constituencies in the GOP camp.)

Philosophical purists, especially outside observers, may find my personal account confusing and disturbing; I acknowledge that there are powerful legacies that constrain the progressive course of Southern politics. Most pertinently, this region disproportionately bears the stubborn, overlapped, negative imprint of America's racial and economic past. Southern politicians, like those of other areas, naturally pander to their base constituencies—whites for the Republicans and blacks for the Democrats—and this tendency can take uncivic character in the social, cultural, economic, and demographic context of Southern political heritage. Unsavory politicking is particularly obvious and brazen in Deep South areas with historic tensions, large numbers of minorities, significant poverty, and opportunistic politicians.

Nevertheless, it is clear that race-based considerations have assumed a certain level of acceptability, prominence, and functionality in the real politics and continuing game of contemporary Southern democracy. In many ways and places, as will be evidenced in the following section, this can be a positive development.

Progressing and Regressing in the New Racial System

In my opinion, the new arrangement represents remarkable adjustment and a new world of biracial and party politics for the South. White and black Southerners now are experiencing a logical normalization of partisan politics—mainly along ideological lines but also reflecting social, and economic patterns—similar to that of the rest of the country.

Ideological Transformation of Regional and National Patterns

Earl Black and Merle Black have captured the essence of this new world of Southern politics—and the national political system—in their comprehensive analysis in *Divided America: The Ferocious Power Struggle in American Politics* (2007):

> The ideological composition of the two Southern parties is very differ-
> ent. African Americans, Latinos, other ethnic groups, and white liberals
> now make up a larger majority of Southern Democrats. The liberal wing

of the party outnumbers the moderate wing, and white conservatives are about as scarce among Southern Democrats as racial minorities were fifty years ago. Just as the Democrats have become more liberal, the Southern Republicans have become more conservative. They attracted the Goldwater voters from the 1960s, and their move forward came when they began to organize the evangelical Christian churches in the 1980s. They are certainly more conservative than the Republican Party of the 1950s.[86]

This transformation of Southern politics has created a "new American regionalism" and a "relentless power struggle" in which the two national parties are decidedly and ideologically different. In all five regions, they report, "Ideological purity within the Democratic Party is matched by ideological purity within the Republican Party."[87]

In summary, they argue:

> The changing composition of the national Democratic and Republican parties is one of the most important stories of modern American politics . . . Changes in party composition have contributed mightily to the ideological purification of modern American politics . . . America's power struggle is rooted in the very different values and priorities advocated by the leading groups in each party's distinctive regional strongholds.[88]

The Alabama Example of Party and Racial Transformation

Accordingly, Alabama politics quite often reflects broader national patterns, with Republicans (mainly whites) articulating conservative-moderate positions and Democrats (including most blacks) taking the moderate-progressive course.

Obviously, racism sometimes contaminates conservatism. Generally speaking, though, these racial considerations are now secondary and supplementary to the broader political mixture of personalities, issues, interests, demographics, and regional networks; overt racial activities seem to be restricted to localized situations in predictable parts of the state.

Most Alabama elections for governor and other state officials during the recent past have been conducted in communitarian language with only sporadic incidence of racist rants or antics.

Alabama governance is normally conducted without patent discrimination, although race-related problems inevitably arise and the federal government keeps an active presence in the state. Moreover, for the most part, Alabamians now conduct regional and local politics in similarly race-conscious but relatively restrained manner. Raceless elections are fairly common, and sometimes amazing situations of "anti-race" politics develop at the local level.

One of the more interesting recent stories, for example, was the election of African American James Fields to the Alabama legislature from virtually all-white Cullman County. Fields, a Democrat, captured 59 percent of the vote in a special election in 2008; by contrast, John McCain carried that Republican stronghold with 82 percent in the November presidential balloting. Even the *New York Times* noted the "historic" nature of "this milestone" in a state "once synonymous with racial strife."[89] While *Times* reporter Adam Nossiter pondered what he termed the "awkwardness of the moment," there was little doubt about the upbeat attitude in a county long tagged as white-man's country:

> "Really, I never realize he's black?" said a smiling white woman in a restaurant.
>
> "He's black?" jokingly asked a white Cullman police officer.
>
> "You know, I don't even see him as black," said a local politician.
>
> Fields himself said "Sometimes I have to pinch myself: 'Am I really black?'"

More consequential is Jerome Gray's account of working with local white officials on progressive electoral adjustments in various parts of Alabama during the 1990s. Gray, field director for many years of the Alabama Democratic Conference, reported impressive success in getting some locales—under pressure from ADC lawsuits and the U.S. Justice Department—to accept alternative experiments for dealing with racial problems.[90] In his published report, Gray summarized: "Once a stronghold of the confederate South,

Alabama is now leading the nation with innovative strategies to correct past wrongs rooted in racism and divisiveness."[91]

Dr. Jess Brown, a political scientist who lives in Huntsville and teaches at Athens State University, explains that many Alabamians—particularly younger people in north Alabama—simply have gotten beyond racial arguments and racial divisions of a bygone era. "It seems to be a generational phenomenon," he told me recently:

> Blacks and whites under thirty have grown up and have been socialized in a different world than those over sixty. I don't think the new generation pays much attention to the noisy crowd from the old days, particularly those leaders who earned their scars in the civil rights movement and see every situation as black and white and try to make every issue and outcome fit their racial experiences. The younger folks just want to make the system work for themselves and their local people. I've seen so many young black and white education and business professionals in our area sit down and deal realistically with the problems of their communities—many of which relate to race—without divisive race talk and turf wars.[92]

Of course, examples of racial regression abound in the recent past—particularly in the arena of campaign politics. Republican Governor Guy Hunt won re-election in 1990 after tying Democratic opponent Paul Hubbert with prominent black leader Joe Reed. Fob James, another Republican, won the gubernatorial election in 1994 after criticizing Democrat Jim Folsom Jr., for allowing removal of the Confederate flag from the capitol building. In partisan turnaround, a public spat with Joe Reed, the aforementioned black leader, probably helped Democrat Don Siegelman defeat James for the governorship in 1998.

Just this year, according to the *Anniston Star*, a neophyte politician shocked both whites and blacks in majority-white Anniston in declaring that he had won the mayor's race by buying the African American vote: "I bought into the black corruption in Anniston. And it worked."[93] Gene Robinson reportedly paid two local black activists $2,650 to round up African American voters on his behalf; and his 3-1 margin in predominantly black areas gave him a stunning 52 percent to 48 percent victory. The black activists confirmed their service to his campaign.

Star reporter Megan Nichols quoted Robinson explaining that he had been offered the black vote for a price during his unsuccessful campaign four years ago, but he had refused that opportunity. "I said no in 2004; but I wanted to win so bad this year."

Robinson later told me that he had not won that election through corruption and that he should have been clearer in his public comments; he also pledged that he will champion biracial progress as the new Anniston mayor. This incident suggests that old-fashioned race-games still lurk in the shadows of contemporary Southern politics.[94]

Ironically, the most flagrant retro race-gaming in contemporary Alabama politics often comes from competition within the black community. A prime case was the 2007 mayoral campaign in Birmingham, a three-fourths black city where black politicians and activists attacked each other with race-based vengeance.

Several major candidates—Larry Langford, the eventual winner who was supported mainly by blacks, Patrick Cooper, the runner-up supported by whites, and embattled incumbent Bernard Kincaid, whose support had shrunk across the board—publicly disavowed racist campaigning; however, their surrogates eagerly railed on this factor. Tom Spencer of the *Birmingham News* captured the tone of this campaign in an analysis immediately preceding the election:[95]

> As the Birmingham mayor's race heats up, supporters of various candidates are wielding the race issue as a weapon, even though all the leading candidates are black.
>
> In an attempt to appeal to blacks, supporters for various campaigns have stepped up attacks, attempting to link their rivals to whites.
>
> Kamau Afrika, a Cooper supporter, has widely distributed a "rap sheet" that slams County Commissioner Langford for the white business support he attracted in previous posts and describes him as a "compromised puppet."
>
> In articles for his Web site, voternewsnetwork.com, and in the *Bir-*

mingham Times, Donald Watkins, a supporter of mayor Bernard Kincaid, charges there is a media conspiracy involving the *Birmingham News* and "Over the Mountain overlords" to promote Cooper. Watkins calls for black unity to resist the "siege."

The most blatant racial appeals have come from radio personality Frank Matthews, a Langford supporter, who unleashed a barrage of race-based rhetoric targeting Cooper. On a nearly nightly basis, Matthews mocks Cooper on his radio talk show as "Mr. Impersonating-The-White-Man Patrick Cooper" and points to campaign donations from white suburbanites. He repeatedly mentions that Cooper's ex-wife is white, a fact he believes is relevant to some voters.

In the city where Dr. Martin Luther King Jr. penned his jailhouse letter and where Dr. Richard Arrington helped pivot Southern history in new directions, the recent campaign was a textbook example of cynical, racial politics. Fortunately, such developments are decreasingly fashionable.

Electon 2008 and Its Meaning for Southern Political History

Election 2008 provides a useful illustration of the current state of affairs—at least for Southern participation in presidential elections and national politics. Certainly, that election was not a good experience for the South; consequently, some have simplistically criticized Southern racism and gloated about the isolation of the region from the American mainstream. Already, the *New York Times* has pronounced the South's waning hold on national politics:[96]

> What may have ended on Election Day, though, is the centrality of the South to national politics. By voting so emphatically for Senator John McCain over Mr. Obama—supporting him in some areas in even greater numbers than they did President Bush—voters from Texas to South Carolina and Kentucky may have marginalized their region for some time to come, political experts say . . .
>
> That could spell the end of the so-called Southern strategy, the doctrine

that took shape under President Richard M. Nixon in which national elections were won by co-opting Southern whites on racial issues. And the Southernization of American politics—which reached its apogee in the 1990s when many Congressional leaders and President Bill Clinton were from the South—appears to have ended.

There's some truth in such pronouncements; but this story misses the mark in equating "redness" with racism. There obviously is some overlap—but tritely depicting the two dimensions as a single phenomenon is both sloppy and wrong.

The South may indeed have isolated itself in national elections—but this is partisan, ideological, philosophical, and cultural regionalization as much as or more so than simple white opposition to a black president. The important development to note is that, over the recent past, Southern politics has shifted toward broader class considerations—factors that sometimes mirror its historical racial system but just as often reflect contemporary social interests and economic differences between black and white societies. The South's white majority consequently inclines toward the Republicans and its black minority aligns almost totally with the Democrats. I'm convinced that, while racism is still "a" driving force, it is no longer "the" driving force in Southern elections or regional black-white relations.

In Alabama, for example, race was an essential, contextual factor in 2008; and partisan forces worked to maximize base constituencies with sophisticated messages and campaigns. As expected, voters here divided along partisan lines in favor of Republican John McCain by a margin of 60 percent to 39 percent, with about eight of every ten whites going for McCain and virtually all blacks picking Obama. It was ugly race/party polarization that reflected poorly on Alabama in many circles; but neither whites nor blacks in this state considered it a perversion of democracy. Many voted "red" and fewer voted "blue"; and nobody seemed overly upset in a state that once was a center of racist resistance and violence.

Polling right after that historic election reflected Alabama's evolving, ambivalent political persona. According to a *Mobile Press-Register*/University of South Alabama survey, Alabamians were generally upbeat about the first

African American President.[97] A majority (54 percent) was either enthusiastic or optimistic about the Obama administration; and a similar majority thought he would help unite rather than divide the country. However, there were racial divisions within these numbers; blacks were overwhelmingly optimistic or enthusiastic (96 percent), while whites were fearful and pessimistic (57 percent). Of course, the poll revealed what everyone knew about a racially divided Alabama; but it also showed that the days of raw racist politicking are pretty much a thing of the past.

Just as pertinent to our discussion is the fact is that Election 2008 says little about black-white relations within the Southern region; and it masks new order alignments on specific issues and programs. Even while polarizing in national elections, Southern whites and blacks have accommodated themselves to functional co-existence in state and local affairs.

Apparently, white and black Southerners now are experiencing a rational regional alignment with the national parties, a logical normalization of politics similar to that of the rest of the nation. In that process of rational nationalization, both Southern politics and American democracy are being transformed; the United States is developing a real two-party system based on regional politics. And the new order is simply an evolving, regionalized part of that system.

The New Racial System: "Workin Jus Fine" for Now for Many Southerners

It is clear that the contemporary scene in Alabama and the South constitutes a New Racial System.

Race and racism continue to be an important force impacting electoral outcomes and the priorities of governance; however, this factor no longer dominates as the perverse, oppressive, all-ruling essence of politics in this part of the country. The race game today is more sophisticated, functional, and accepted—by both whites and blacks.

The contemporary version of "real Southern politics" is not a very inspired or inspiring solution to the South's historic racial dilemma; and there are still too many ugly, painful, cankerous sores on the South's political body. But, considering our legacy of hard history, the New Racial System may be functional for this stage of evolving political history. To use a Southern colloquialism, it seems to be "workin jus fine" for now for a lot of people— white and black. At least they can live, and work, and talk together; and therein may lie the potential for future progress.

V

Hard History and Contemporary Southern Politics

So, WHAT CAN WE learn from this interpretive analysis of changing Southern politics?

(1) THE CONTINUING "RACE GAME" IN SOUTHERN POLITICS.

Of course, the obvious reality of any discussion about Southern politics is still the continuing, stubborn power of race and racism. The Southern race game endures. Both races now play the game; regional concerns have shifted to more conventional issues and practices; but politics inside the belly of the Southern beast still relates in troubling ways to matters of black and white. Enough said on this point.

(2) "REAL SOUTHERN POLITICS" AND SYSTEMIC EVOLUTION.

The concept of "real Southern politics" has proven valuable in studying the South's evolving course over the past half-century. Inside scrutiny of elusive dealings between white and black politicos helps explain the moderating nature, activities, and outcomes of Southern politics since the civil rights movement. It is possible, furthermore, that the Southern political system will evolve in more progressive directions in the future; and "real" insights may seem less striking, less instructive, and less interesting in the less peculiar race game of the changing South.

I suspect, however, that "real Southern politics" will continue as a distinguishing regional trademark for many years to come. As William Faulkner might say, the Southern racial beast lives on because neither white nor black Southerners will let it die.

(3) "A New Racial System" of Cultural Accommodation.

Perhaps the most important theoretical finding is the "New Racial System" of contemporary politics. Southern politics—although still racked with racial problems—is more open, candid, and accepted in great part because the two races have mutually accommodated progress, practicality, and cherished sensitivities of black and white culture in this region. Race is still pervasive, and, in some places at some times, race relations regress toward the olden ways. But there definitely is a new regime of "accommodation" between blacks and whites; the Southern race game is more biracial, positive, and functional—in substance, style, strategy, operations, and outcomes—than ever before.

The validity of this analysis obviously awaits the judgment of further scrutiny and history. As mentioned in an earlier discussion, current public officials are reluctant and perhaps unreliable witnesses to the new racial politics; however, I have asked two knowledgeable and candid observers—one white and one black—to assess my idea about evolving Southern politics. While their comments present nuanced perspectives about the substantive sufficiency of the contemporary order, each endorses the thesis of a new racial politics in the South.

Dr. Artemesia Stanberry, assistant professor of political science at North Carolina Central University, is an Alabama native with extensive experience as a staff assistant for several Southern members of Congress. She began her Washington career in my office; we have worked together on other research relating to Southern politics. Stanberry agrees with the depiction of a new racial system:

> This study fills a gap with the inside story of the South's halfway house of racialized politics. Obviously, something important and heretofore unnoted happened after the rabid racism of George Wallace and the righteous indignation of Dr. King; and that "something" is the biracial alliance depicted here. There is no doubt that this region has come a

long way from open antagonisms of the past. What we see is significant movement toward a new arrangement where black politicians and groups engage alongside their white counterparts. Black minorities now participate and their concerns sometimes take center stage in contemporary public life. Overt race-gaming has been relegated, for the most part, to a more sophisticated politics that avoids the divisions of yesteryear and makes the Southern system functional.

However, she cautions about the optimistic definitiveness and connotation of my depiction:

Today's game still unduly favors white majorities and their conservative priorities; and there are far too many disparities in Southern life and society. The South clearly has made progress—but there is a long way to go.

Dr. Paul Hubbert, executive director of the Alabama Education Association and arguably the most powerful influence in Alabama politics during the past few decades, says that this analysis explains much of the "cultural schizophrenia" and "partisan polarization" in the region; but he also sees progress in the South's new racial politics:

Times are changing in the South, and this interpretation of the difference in attitude between young and old Southerners seems to be an accurate picture of the change that has and will continue to occur. Particularly interesting is the noted difference between young and old Southerners. As gradual as this process seems to be, there is a march in Alabama and the other Southern states toward a society where one's status is based more on merit than on the color of one's skin. This manuscript seems to catch the essence of that slow but steady movement.[99]

Thus, the new way of conducting regional political life is not much to brag about, but it works better than anything we have ever tried before. Southern politics will continue as a peculiar regional practice; but the raw, racial conflict and rhetoric of the past have softened considerably. Perhaps now is the time to talk about moving further along the road toward racial conciliation.

A CALL FOR FURTHER STUDY OF THE NEW RACIAL SYSTEM

In this original thesis, I have attempted to provide a new interpretation of Southern politics as we begin a new century. I've presented an unusual analysis of real Southern politics of the past and heralded the New Racial System of more sophisticated, still race-racked, but somewhat normalizing politics.

Now I would like to proceed with some reflective ideas that do not fit the 1-2-3 flow of my conclusions but that I consider worth discussing here at the end of this manuscript.

I want to encourage my academic associates to pursue the New Racial System—with an open, balanced, inquisitive approach.

TIME FOR "NEW HISTORIES" AND CONTEMPORARY ANALYSIS

It may be time, as historian Charles Eagles argued in a survey of the literature, for academics to explore "new histories" challenging the established story line and extending analysis forward in more balanced, even iconoclastic directions.[98] Historian Glenn Feldman has suggested, furthermore, that scholars should constrain passionate sentiments and political correctness in future research on Southern history; "Those convictions may make good politics and good social policy, but they do not always make good history."[99] We know aplenty about the "heroic drama" of the civil rights movement and post-movement struggles. It is time to reexamine and expand what we "know"; and, perhaps more urgently, we need to try to understand the New Racial System of the twenty-first century.

GRAPPLE WITH RACE AS A REALITY IN SOUTHERN POLITICS

I also agree with political scientist Richard K. Scher that our discipline needs to contribute more substantively to the literature on current racial politics. In a recent review, Scher recommended that we grapple with race and assess how it impacts on Southern politics in real-world terms instead of as a cold, independent variable for statistical models: "Race is a fundamental element in American politics in exactly the same way V. O. Key saw it as fundamental to Southern politics more than fifty years ago."[100]

CONTRIBUTE SOMETHING TO AMERICAN DEMOCRACY

Perhaps today's political leaders and journalists might learn something from studying the New Racial System. As my colleagues Lucius J. Barker, Mack Jones, and Katherine Tate observe in their analysis of racial politics in the American democratic system:

> . . . we need to know more about the behavior and responsiveness of elected white officials from districts where there are very large and discrete black and minority populations. Conversely, we need to know how black members of Congress deal with the matter of representing white populations in their districts. Given the historical and contemporary context of racial politics and race relations in this country, along with the thorny conceptual issues surrounding political representation more generally, answering this question could prove difficult for any representative, regardless of race or ethnicity. But we suggest that precisely those representatives who are able to overcome such difficulties will do much to improve both race relations and the overall quality of life in this country.[101]

A BROADER CHALLENGE TO THE AMERICAN DILEMMA

I also believe that the good faith people of this region might help America work its way through the shameful dilemma of national racial history. Perhaps there is something constructive, and more broadly useful, in this region's current and candid approach to matters of black and white relations. After all, the race game is not limited to the South.

THE RACE GAME OF AMERICAN DEMOCRACY

I intend this assertion as a blunt reminder that racism is a national problem. Our discomforting discussion in this book of the South's racial situation should lead inevitably to an equally discomforting discussion about what Gunnar Myrdal called "America's dilemma" six decades ago.[102]

According to my analysis, the Southern political system has changed substantially over the past half-century. This region is ideologically "redder" than most; but it has evolved beyond racial perversities and contortions of the Old South. Race relations in this part of the country are still problematic; but the regional situation now is simply a more obvious and intense case of the American racial problem. Perhaps the time has come for the South and America to talk as a nation about our common situation.

It is awkward and difficult for a Southerner to raise this issue; so I will let outsiders address the problem of the national race game before I offer my bold invitation to Barack Obama.

First is Thomas Sugrue, a Detroit native and University of Pennsylvania historian. In an almost encyclopedic volume on the northern civil rights movement, Sugrue recently noted the problematic consequence of conventional history's focus on the heroic drama in the South:[103]

> Though the differences between North and South were real, our emphasis on Southern exceptionalism has led historians, journalists, and political commentators to overlook the commonalities across regions. The long and well-publicized history of racial atrocities in the South gave northerners a badge of honor, a sense that they were not part of America's troubled racial history.[104]

Racial inequalities—both before and after the movement—took different form and nature on the two sides of the Mason-Dixon line, Sugrue argued; and he replicated Myrdal's indictment for the twenty-first century:

> While the situation of blacks—North and South—was unmistakably better at the turn of the twenty-first century than it had been at the turn of the twentieth, the history of the black freedom struggle, especially in the North, is not just one of victories. It is full of paradoxes and ambiguities, of unfinished battles and devastating defeats.[105]

Sugrue also provided convincing evidence for his regional assertion:

> At the opening of the twenty-first century, the fifteen most segre-

gated metropolitan areas in the United States were in the Northeast and Midwest. A half century after the Supreme Court struck down separate, unequal schools as unconstitutional, racial segregation is still the norm in northern public schools. The five states with the highest rates of school segregation—New York, New Jersey, Illinois, Michigan, and California— are all outside the South. Rates of unemployment, underemployment, and poverty reach Third World levels among African Americans in nearly every major northern city, where the faces in welfare offices, unemployment lines, homeless shelters, and jails are disproportionately black.[106]

Furthermore, Brooklyn-based, Berkeley-educated journalist Jacob Levenson has concluded that, for most outsiders, the South serves mainly to make America feel comfortable with its racial dilemma.[107] After spending time in Alabama researching AIDS among blacks, he wrote:

> Nobody seems to know exactly what to make of the South anymore . . . When we do think of it, it is often frozen in time: Martin Luther King Jr. marching on Selma or [Birmingham Police Commissioner] Bull Connor's men spraying fire hoses on civil rights marchers. Those are the images rehashed on PBS, anyway. Strangely, we seem to treasure those black-and-white memories, and when we drag them out, we do it with a sort of pride. It's as if they remind and reassure us that we are a people who will stare down hatred and injustice. They serve as symbols of what we'd like to think we're not.[108]

Levenson said that, for most Americans, the South is a place that is distinct from the rest of the country:

> Yet these images are useful in this respect only to the extent that we believe that "the South" is somehow a place that exists culturally, socially, and physically apart from the rest of the country. This strikes me as a provincial and largely artificial conceit. The South, with its fine-tuned sense of civility, self-determination, and morality has always powerfully mirrored our national character. And it remains a startling, beautiful,

complex, and in many ways revealing reflection of America and what we've become.[109]

In a sense, Levenson suggested, stereotyping the South actually limits our commitment to a bolder agenda as a nation:

> The difficulty with this enterprise is that the South is still often cast as completely other. So . . . talking about race in the South becomes a way of not talking about race in the rest of the country. It's a point worth highlighting, and it extends beyond race . . . the political horse race stories that can casually frame God, guns, and gays as Southern concerns promise to oversimplify Southerners' relationship to these issues, and, at the same time, relegate the national struggle to come to terms with these same issues to the periphery of the debate.[110]

Levenson went on to say that the South offers the nation an opportunity to recognize and address its own dark issues:

> ". . . it strikes me that one of the basic tensions that threads its way through many Southern stories has to do with whether the region is still chained to its racial past, or whether it has reached catharsis, redeemed itself, and joined the rest of the country . . . I would suggest just the opposite, that the South is on the leading edge of a whole series of stories that are vital to the rest of the country because it has been forced, largely by virtue of its racial past, to publicly confront issues that the rest of the nation has been able to avoid.[111]

Certainly, neither Sugrue nor Levenson is a fan of Dixie, the Southern race game, or real Southern politics. However, their works should be required reading for Southerners and non-Southerners alike who are trying to make sense of the peculiar South and the continuing challenge of race in America.

"WELCOME TO THE SOUTH," PRESIDENT BARACK OBAMA

Thus perhaps it would be a good idea for Barack Obama, the first African American president, to proceed expeditiously with his national dialogue on race—and he's welcome to begin in the South. I suggest he come to Alabama and talk with people of both races, some of whom participated in V. O. Key's study a half-century ago, many who still remember the days of George Wallace and Martin Luther King, and countless others young enough to respond to the president's oft-expressed commitment to racial reconciliation.[112]

The idea of presidential necessity may have enflamed racial tensions on the campaign trail, but such leadership is required if we are ever going to confront the national race game of American history. The truth is that Barack Obama is especially qualified—as an African American president inside the "real politics" and "race game" of American democracy—to chart the course of racial reconciliation. And that course could begin in Alabama.

This is not one of my weird, exaggerated scenarios imagined earlier in the fanciful introduction to the South's New Racial System. I'm not naïve enough to think that we have any magical answers or that Obama has mystical powers. But convening in the Cradle of the Confederacy and the birthplace of the civil rights movement, in such a ripe and poignant time, we might be able to do something incredibly good for ourselves and America.

President Obama should seriously consider this invitation. He alone can craft a new affirmative "Southern strategy" as we try, along with the rest of the country, to evolve our racial order in more positive and less cynical ways for a new century.

In summary, we have observed in this analysis that the South seems to be taking some clumsy steps forward in the New Racial System of the twenty-first century. In some areas, the new politics suggests progress; on the other hand, the path has proven rocky in locales burdened with hard history, large black populations, endemic poverty, and opportunistic politicians. Of course, whether the new order constitutes real and significant progress in the Southern race game (or simply cynical adjustment of real Southern politics) is a matter of personal perspective; and future developments will shape the judgment of history.

I did not know the righteous Dr. King, but I figure from reading his books and speeches that he would see some positives in the New Racial System. I did know the repentant Governor Wallace, and I figure he too would welcome some developments as recounted in this manuscript. I imagine Professor Key (whom I never met but whose works I've studied and taught *ad tedium* for most of my adult life) might say: "I didn't anticipate such developments, but it makes some sense considering Southern political history."

I'm also confident that, after due consideration, they would view the glass as half-full rather than half-empty; and they would demand that we try harder to fill the vessel of Southern democracy.

Finally, I'm convinced that Reverend King, Governor Wallace, and Professor Key would join me in urging President Obama to conduct his national dialogue for racial reconciliation here in Alabama at the crossroads of civil war and civil rights.

Notes

1   Stephan Lesher, *George Wallace: American Populist* (Addison-Wesley, 1994), p. 174.

2   Martin Luther King Jr. *The Words of Martin Luther King, Jr., Selected by Coretta Scott King* (Newmarket, 1984), p. 95.

3   For classic reading on race and Southern political history, I suggest: W. J. Cash, *The Mind of the South* (Knopf, 1941); V. O. Key Jr., *Southern Politics in State and Nation* (Knopf, 1949); C. Vann Woodward, *The Strange Career of Jim Crow* (Oxford University Press, 1955). I also recommend, as a contemporary and alternative perspective, Manning Marable's *Race, Reform, and Rebellion: The Second Reconstruction and Beyond in Black America, 1945–2006* (University Press of Mississippi, 2007). Readers will also find among these endnotes a representative sample of other interesting and useful books from early classics to modern perspectives.

4   My credentials include intermingled careers in academics and politics. I am now retired and affiliated with Jacksonville State University as Professor Emeritus in American Democracy. My association with JSU—mainly as a political science professor—stretches back to 1971. I also served in the Alabama Legislature (1982–86), as Alabama Secretary of State (1987–89), and as a U.S. Congressman (1989–97). Interested persons can access additional and relevant material in the Browder Collection at JSU in Alabama. Or consult Geni Certain, with Glen Browder, *Professor-Politician* (forthcoming from NewSouth Books, 2009).

5   Clearly my "original analysis" incorporates the contributions of others. For example, James M. Glaser's fieldwork on Southern political campaigns—including my first congressional campaign—evidenced evolving racial strategies in the South. See *Race, Campaign Politics, & the Realignment in the South* (Yale University Press, 1996); and *The Hand of the Past in Contemporary Southern Politics* (Yale University Press, 2005). Also, Matthew J. Streb identified the altered role of racial rhetoric in Southern and national

elections; see *The New Electoral Politics of Race* (University of Alabama Press, 2002). The works of these and other scholars figure prominently in my thesis about the New Racial System.

6   I agree with Richard K. Scher, who recently complained that political scientists usually neglect this aspect of Southern politics: "Regardless of what theoretical and normative perspectives are used, political scientists need to enter the study of the civil rights movement, and of race generally, more vigorously than they have. Race is not simply an independent variable that political scientists can manipulate to suit the needs of sophisticated, *au courant* statistical models they choose to employ in their research. Race is a fundamental element in American politics in exactly the same way V. O. Key saw it as fundamental to Southern politics more than fifty years ago." See Richard K. Scher, "Unfinished Business: Writing the Civil Rights Movement," in *Writing Southern Politics*, edited by Robert P. Steed and Laurence W. Moreland (University Press of Kentucky, 2006), p. 88.

7   Several historians have called for new approaches to Southern political history. For example, see Charles W. Eagles, "Toward New Histories of the Civil Rights Era," *Journal of Southern History* 66 (November 2000): pp. 845–48; and Glenn Feldman, *Reading Southern History: Essays on Interpreters and Interpretations* (University of Alabama Press, 2001), p. 11.

8   Consult note 26 and other citations in this manuscript for material on Southern transformation over the past half-century.

9   This analysis would be different if written, for example, by a black scholar/politician; perhaps someone will respond with the African American perspective on the race game and real Southern politics. Until then, the reader may want to consult the following sources:

   • Lucius J. Barker, Mack Jones, and Katherine Tate, *African Americans and the American Political System* (Prentice Hall. 1998).

   • Ralph C. Gomes and Linda Faye Williams, *From Exclusion to Inclusion: The Long Struggle for African American Political Power* (Praeger, 1995).

   • Manning Marable, *Race, Reform, and Rebellion: The Second Reconstruction and Beyond in Black America 1945–2006* (University Press of Mississippi, 2007).

   • Huey L. Perry (ed.), *Race, Politics and Governance in the United States* (University Press of Florida, 1996).

   • Georgia A. Persons (ed.), *Dilemmas of Black Politics: Issues of Leadership and Strategy* (HarperCollins College Division, 1993).

   • Ronald W. Walters and Robert C. Smith, *African American Leadership* (State University of New York Press, 1999).

   • Hanes Walton and Robert C. Smith. *American Politics and the African American Quest for Universal Freedom* (Longman, 2009).

10 There are countless books on the "heroic drama" of the civil rights move-
    ment and Southern politics of that period. I suggest the following sources
    for diverse and representative coverage. Some have particular pertinence to
    Alabama:

- Richard Arrington Jr., *There's Hope for the World: The Memoir of Birming-
  ham, Alabama's First African American Mayor* (University of Alabama
  Press, 2008).
- Taylor Branch, *Parting the Waters: America in the King Years* (Simon
  & Schuster, 1988); *Pillar of Fire: America in the King Years* (Simon &
  Schuster, 1998); *At Canaan's Edge: America in the King Years*, 1965–68
  (Simon & Schuster, 2006).
- Clayborne Carson (ed.), *The Autobiography of Martin Luther King, Jr.*
  (Warner Books, 1998).
- Dan Carter, *The Politics of Rage: George Wallace, the Origins of the New
  Conservatism, and the Transformation of American Politics* (Louisiana State
  University Press, 2000).
- William H. Chafe, *Civilities and Civil Rights: Greensboro, North Carolina,
  and the Black Struggle for Freedom* (Oxford University Press, 1980).
- David L. Chappell, *Inside Agitators: White Southerners in the Civil Rights
  Movement* (Johns Hopkins University Press, 1994).
- J. L. Chestnut Jr. and Julia Cass, *Black in Selma: The Uncommon Life of J.
  L. Chestnut, Jr.* (Farrar, Straus and Giroux, 1990).
- Charles W. Eagles, *The Civil Rights Movement in America: Essays* (Univer-
  sity Press of Mississippi, 1986).
- Glenn T. Eskew, *But for Birmingham: The Local and National Movements
  in the Civil Rights Struggle* (University of North Carolina Press, 1997).
- Glenn Feldman, *Before Brown: Civil Rights and White Backlash in the
  Modern South* (University of Alabama Press, 2004).
- Wayne Flynt, *Alabama in the Twentieth Century: The Modern South* (Uni-
  versity of Alabama Press, 2006).
- David J. Garrow, *Bearing the Cross: Martin Luther King, Jr., and the
  Southern Christian Leadership Conference* (Morrow, 1986).
- Robert S. Graetz, *A White Preacher's Message on Race and Reconciliation:
  Based on His Experiences Beginning with the Montgomery Bus Boycott*
  (NewSouth Books, 2006).
- Carl Grafton and Anne Permaloff, *Big Mules and Branchheads: James
  E. Folsom and Political Power in Alabama* (University of Georgia Press,
  1985).
- Fred D. Gray, *Bus Ride to Justice: The Life and Works of Fred Gray*
  (NewSouth Books, 2003.

- John Hayman, with Clara Ruth Hayman, *A Judge in the Senate: Howell Heflin's Career of Politics and Principle* (NewSouth Books, 2001).
- Harvey H. Jackson, *Inside Alabama: A Personal History of My State* (University of Alabama Press, 2004).
- Martin Luther King Jr., *Where Do We Go From Here: Chaos or Community* (Harper and Row, 1967).
- Stephan Lesher, *George Wallace: American Populist* (Addison-Wesley Publishing Company, 1994).
- John Lewis and Michael D'Orso, *Walking with the Wind: A Memoir of the Movement* (Simon & Schuster, 1998).
- Andrew M. Manis, *A Fire You Can't Put Out: The Civil Rights Life of Birmingham's Reverend Fred Shuttlesworth* (University of Alabama Press, 1999).
- Manning Marable, *Race, Reform and Rebellion: The Second Reconstruction and Beyond in Black America, 1945–2006* (University Press of Mississippi, 2007).
- Diane McWhorter, *Carry Me Home: Birmingham, Alabama; The Climactic Battle of the Civil Rights Revolution* (Simon & Schuster, 2001).
- J. Phillips Noble, *Beyond the Burning Bus: The Civil Rights Revolution in a Southern Town* (NewSouth Books, 2003).
- Rosa Parks, with Jim Haskins, *Rosa Parks: My Story* (Dial Books, 1992).
- Gene Roberts and Hank Klibanoff, *The Race Beat: The Press, the Civil Rights Struggle; and the Awakening of a Nation* (Knopf, 2006).
- William Warren Rogers, Robert David Ward, Leah Rawls Atkins, and Wayne Flynt, *Alabama: The History of a Deep South State* (University of Alabama Press, 1994).
- Solomon S. Seay and Delores R. Boyd, *Jim Crow and Me: Stories from My Life as a Civil Rights Lawyer* (NewSouth Books, 2009).
- Frank Sikora, *The Judge: The Life and Opinions of Alabama's Frank M. Johnson, Jr.* (NewSouth Books, 2007).
- Jason Sokol, *There Goes My Everything: White Southerners in the Age of Civil Rights, 1945–1975* (Vintage, 2007).
- Steve Suitts, *Hugo Black of Alabama: How His Roots and Early Career Shaped the Great Champion of the Constitution* (NewSouth Books, 2005).
- J. Mills Thornton III, *Dividing Lines: Municipal Politics and the Struggle for Civil Rights in Montgomery, Birmingham, and Selma* (University of Alabama Press, 2002).
- Warren Trest, *Nobody But the People: The Life and Times of Alabama's Youngest Governor* (NewSouth Books, 2008).

- Juan Williams, *Eyes on the Prize: America's Civil Rights Years, 1954–1965* (Penguin Books, 1987).

11   There are many accounts of the South's historical race problem. Consult notes 9, 10, 26, 32 and other citations throughout this manuscript.

12   Richard K. Cralle, *The Works of John C. Calhoun, Vol. II* (Russell & Russell, 1968). pp. 625–33.

13   For a concise but interesting account of the 1901 convention and constitutional history in Alabama, see Dana Beyerle, "How The Constitution Came To Be: It's Quite a Birthday for a Document Steeped in Alabama's History," *Tuscaloosa News,* November 18, 2001.

14   V. O. Key Jr., *Southern Politics in State and Nation* (Alfred A. Knopf, 1949).

15   Ibid, p. 4.

16   Ibid, p. 361.

17   Donald R. Matthews and James W. Prothro, *Negroes and the New Southern Politics,* (Harcourt, Brace and World, 1966).

18   Ibid, p. 334.

19   Earl Black and Merle Black, *Politics and Society in the South* (Harvard University Press, 1987).

20   Ibid, pp. 127–33.

21   Richard K. Scher, *Politics in the New South: Republicanism, Race, and Leadership in the Twentieth Century* (Sharpe, 1997).

22   Ibid, pp. 228-30.

23   Ibid, p. 230.

24   William R. Keech, *The Impact of Negro Voting: The Role of the Vote in the Quest for Equality* (Greenwood, 1968).

25   Ibid, p. 109.

26   For representative scholarship on systemic transformation, consult the following sources:

- Numan V. Bartley and Hugh Davis Graham, *Southern Politics and the Second Reconstruction* (Johns Hopkins University Press, 1975).
- Jack Bass and Walter DeVries, *The Transformation of Southern Politics: Social Change and Political Consequence Since 1945* (University of Georgia Press, 1995).
- Stanley P. Berard, *Southern Democrats in the U.S. House of Representatives* (University of Oklahoma Press, 2001).
- Earl Black and Merle Black, *Divided America: The Ferocious Power Struggle in American Politics* (Simon and Schuster, 2007).
- Charles S. Bullock and Mark J. Rozell, *The New Politics of the Old South:*

An Introduction to Southern Politics (Rowman and Littlefield, 2007).

• Chandler Davidson and Bernard Grofman, *Quiet Revolution in the South: The Impact of the Voting Rights Act, 1965–1990* (Princeton University Press, 1994).

• William C. Havard, *The Changing Politics of the South* (Louisiana State University, 1972).

• Alexander Lamis, *Southern Politics of the 1990s* (Louisiana State University, 1999).

• David Lublin, *The Republican South: Democratization and Partisan Change* (Princeton University Press, 2007).

• Richard K. Scher, *Politics in the New South: Republicanism, Race, and Leadership in the Twentieth Century* (Sharpe, 1997).

• Robert P. Steed, Laurence W. Moreland, and Tod A. Baker. *Southern Parties and Elections: Studies in Regional Political Change* (University of Alabama Press, 1997).

• Matthew J. Streb, *The New Electoral Politics of Race* (University of Alabama Press, 2002).

• Robert H. Swansbrough and David M. Brodsky, *The South's New Politics: Realignment and Dealignment* (University of South Carolina Press, 1988).

• J. David Woodard, *The New Southern Politics* (Lynne Rienner, 2007), p. 169.

27   Earl Black and Merle Black, *The Rise of Southern Republicans* (Belknap, 2002).

28   Ibid, p. 3.

29   Charles S. Bullock and Mark J. Rozell, *The New Politics of the Old South: An Introduction to Southern Politics* (Rowman and Littlefield, 2007).

30   Ibid, pp. 1–2.

31   Ibid, pp.1–2.

32   For recent, representative re-visioning of Southern politics, see the following newspaper articles, listed chronologically: Shaila Dewan, "Southern Blacks Are Split on Clinton vs. Obama," *New York Times*, January 18, 2008; Patricia Cohen, "Interpreting Some Overlooked Stories from the South," *New York Times*, May 1, 2007; Phillip Rawls, "State House and Senate OK Slavery Apologies," Associated Press, April 25, 2007; Tom Gordon, "From Black Belt Roots Grows New Racial View," *Birmingham News*, April 24, 2007; David J. Garrow, "The Klan Is Still Dead," *Los Angeles Times*, February 27, 2007; Shailagh Murray, "A Balancing Act in the Upper South," *Washington Post*, October 9, 2006; Brian Lyman, "The Calculus of Elections," *Anniston Star*, October 15, 2006; and an editorial, "Does Race

Still Matter?" *Anniston Star*, September 6, 2006. Also, for some interesting insights into contemporary life in the Deep South, see the ten-part series by John Fleming on "Economic and Social Justice in Alabama's Black Belt," in the *Anniston Star* (2006).

33   John Fleming; "Selma's Salvation," *Anniston Star*, September 3, 2006.

34   Ibid.

35   Ibid.

36   John Lewis and Michael D'Orso, *Walking with the Wind: A Memoir of the Movement* (Simon & Schuster, 1998).

37   Ibid, pp. 463–64. Lewis qualified his endorsement of changing Southern ways with the following statement: "But there is a mistaken assumption among many that these signs of progress mean that the battle is over, that the struggle for civil rights is finished, that the problems of segregation were solved in the '60s and now all we have to deal with are economic issues. This is preposterous." (p. 464)

38   Fred D. Gray, *Bus Ride to Justice: Changing the System by the System* (Black Belt Press, 1995).

39   Ibid, pp. 355-56. Gray also qualified his positive remarks: "However, one of the most disheartening observations I have made over the years is that most of the persons who made up what we called the white power structure have never gone beyond doing exactly what the courts have ordered. I hope the time will come that elected and appointed officials would treat African Americans fairly, equally, and go beyond the letter of the law to bring about change not because a court ordered them to, but because it's the right thing to do." (pp. 355–56)

40   J. L. Chestnut Jr., and Julia Cass, *Black in Selma: The Uncommon Life of J. L. Chestnut, Jr.* (Farrar, Straus and Giroux, 1990).

41   Ibid, p. 418. Here's Chestnut's qualifier: "We are far from the world envisioned by King in his 'I have a Dream' speech. We are closer to it, but getting there will continue to be a struggle. People forget that King said near the end of that speech, 'I [now] go back to the South'—meaning to implement the dream of freedom and justice for all by marches, boycotts, and other means the establishment detested. I see King, at the expense of his life, striving to realize the dream, not just pleasantly dreaming." (p. 418)

42   Frederick M. Wirt, *"We Ain't What We Was": Civil Rights in the New South* (Duke University Press, 1997), p. 29. Also consult Wirt, *The Politics of Southern Equality: Law and Social Change in a Mississippi County* (Aldine, 1970).

43   My notion of "Southern Democracy" differs from how others have used the term. Earl Black and Merle Black, for example, focus on white South-

ern electoral "preference" for the Democratic Party in national politics; I emphasize white Southerners "using" the Democratic Party for racial dominance in state and local politics. See their chapter on "The Decline of Southern 'Democracy'" in *Politics and Society in the South* (Harvard University Press, 1987).

44 Earl Black and Merle Black, *Divided America: The Ferocious Power Struggle in American Politics* (Simon and Schuster, 2007).

45 George Wallace's presidential exploits clearly represent a contradictory wrinkle in this generalization; but that's another story for another time.

46 I grew up in a time and place and environment of intense national significance—the civil rights revolution—without any apparent passion or personal involvement in that revolution. As I have acknowledged in another manuscript, "I was an acquiescent product of the Deep South culture of class and caste, proceeding through the civil rights revolution with more pressing personal concerns and with conflicted accommodation to the Southern way of life." For a discussion of this aspect of my background, see "Profile of a New Kind of Leader," in the upcoming book by Glen Browder and Artemesia Stanberry, *Stealth Reconstruction: The Untold Story of Southern Political History* (forthcoming from NewSouth Books, 2009).

47 Dan T. Carter, *The Politics of Rage: George Wallace, the Origins of the New Conservatism, and the Transformation of American Politics* (Louisiana State University Press, 1996), pp. 264–93.

48 Ibid, p. 291.

49 John Hayman, *Bitter Harvest: Richmond Flowers and the Civil Rights Revolution* (Black Belt Press, 1996).

50 Ibid, p. 255.

51 Ibid, p. 255.

52 Ibid, pp. 283–287.

53 For further discussion of these races, see Carl Elliott, Sr. and Michael D'Orso *The Cost of Courage: The Journey of an American Congressman* (Doubleday, 1992); and John Hayman, *Bitter Harvest: Richmond Flowers and the Civil Rights Revolution* (Black Belt Press, 1996).

54 Ibid, pp. 256–57.

55 Elliott and D'Orso, pp. 276–82.

56 Donald R. Matthews and James W. Prothro, *Negroes and the New Southern Politics* (Harcourt, Brace, and World, 1966).

57 Ibid, p. 484.

58 Ibid, p. 235.

59 Alfred B. Clubok, John M. De Grove, and Charles D. Farris, "The Manipulated Negro Vote: Some Pre-Conditions and Consequences," *Journal*

of Politics 1964: pp. 112–29.

60   Ibid, pp. 117–19.

61   Ibid, p. 119.

62   Larry J. Sabato and Glenn R. Simpson, *Dirty Little Secrets: The Persistence of Corruption in American Politics* (Times Books, 1996).

63   Ibid, pp. 190–91.

64   Ibid, p. 191.

65   Ibid, pp. 314–15.

66   For a full analysis of quiet, practical, biracial politics, see Glen Browder and Artemesia Stanberry, *Stealth Reconstruction: The Untold Story of Southern Political History* (forthcoming from NewSouth Books, 2009).

67   Ibid.

68   Joe L. Reed, personal interview, August 3, 2007.

69   See John Hayman, with Clara Ruth Hayman, *A Judge in the Senate: Howell Heflin's Career of Politics and Principle* (NewSouth Books, 2001).

70   The voting information reported in this section is derived from several sources; some data represent compilations by the author using original source files. Interested readers can consult documents in the Browder Collection at Jacksonville State University or access online organizations such as Project Vote Smart (www.vote-smart.org).

71   See Glen Browder and Artemesia Stanberry, *Stealth Reconstruction: The Untold Story of Southern Political History* (forthcoming from NewSouth Books, 2009); "Stealth Leadership and Changing Southern Politics During the 1970s-80s-90s: A New Perspective and Exploratory Survey," The Citadel Symposium on Southern Politics, Charleston, South Carolina, March 6, 2008; Glen Browder and Artemesia Stanberry, "Stealth Leadership in Alabama Politics and Southern History: A Congressional Survey and Progress Report," the Alabama Political Science Association Annual Meeting, Mobile, Alabama, March 21, 2008.

72   Richard Arrington, telephone and email communications, April 2008.

73   Jerome Gray, telephone, mail, and email communications, 2007–08.

74   Fred Gray, telephone communication, May 8, 2008.

75   *Birmingham Weekly*, an alternative publication, ran a series on "Alabama's New Racial Order," written by this author, as its cover story in the fall of 2008.

76   Settlement Agreement in *Knight v. Alabama* (2006).

77   Ibid.

78   Ibid.

79   Sara Hebel, "Segregation's Legacy Still Troubles Campuses," *Chronicle of Higher Education*, May 14, 2004.

80   James Salzer and Gayle White, "Lawmaker Suggests Merging Historically Black Colleges," *Atlanta Journal-Constitution*, December 1, 2008.

81   Matthew J. Streb, *The New Electoral Politics of Race* (University of Alabama Press, 2002).

82   Ibid, p.2.

83   Ibid, pp. 200–01.

84   Ibid, pp. 188–205.

85   Ibid, p. 200.

86   Earl Black and Merle Black, *Divided America: The Ferocious Power Struggle in American Politics* (Simon and Schuster, 2007), p. 90.

87   Ibid, p. 254.

88   Ibid, pp. 241, 254–60.

89   Adam Nossiter, "Race Matters Less in Politics of South," *New York Times*, February 21, 2008.

90   Jerome Gray, *Winning Fair Representation in At-Large Elections: Cumulative Voting and Limited Voting in Alabama Local Elections* (limited review edition, Southern Regional Council and the Center for Voting and Democracy, 1999).

91   Ibid, p. 30.

92   Jess Brown, telephone interview, November 9, 2008.

93   Megan Nichols, "Dominating the Polls: 'I Bought into the Black Corruption in Anniston,' Says Robinson," *Anniston Star*, August 28, 2008.

94   Glen Browder, "Buying the Black Vote: Anniston's Candid New Mayor Sends a Bizarre But Useful Message to Alabama and America," *Birmingham Weekly*, September 4, 2008; "A Political Novice May Have Scratched the Scab off Festering Racial Sores in Anniston," *Birmingham News*, September 7, 2008.

95   Tom Spencer, "Race an Issue in Mayoral Battle, Poll Concludes," *Birmingham News*, October 1, 2007.

96   Adam Nossiter, "For South, a Waning Hold on Politics," *New York Times*, November 11, 2008.

97   Sean Reilly, "Poll: State's Reaction to Obama Mixed," *Mobile Press-Register*, November 16, 2008.

98   Charles W. Eagles, "Toward New Histories of the Civil Rights Era," *Journal of Southern History* 66 (November 2000), pp. 845–48.

99   Glenn Feldman, *Reading Southern History: Essays on Interpreters and Interpretations* (University of Alabama Press, 2001), p. 11.

100 Richard K. Scher, "Unfinished Business: Writing the Civil Rights Movement," in *Writing Southern Politics*, edited by Robert P. Steed and Laurence W. Moreland (University Press of Kentucky, 2006), p. 88.

101 Lucius J. Barker, Mack Jones, and Katherine Tate, *African Americans and the American Political System* (Prentice Hall, 1998), pp. 296–97.

102 Gunnar Myrdal, *An American Dilemma: The Negro Problem and Modern Democracy* (Harper and Brothers, 1944).

103 Thomas J. Sugrue, *Sweet Land of Liberty: The Forgotten Struggle for Civil Rights in the North* (Random House, 2008).

104 Ibid, p. xiv.

105 Ibid, p. xix.

106 Ibid.

107 Jacob Levenson, "Divining Dixie: Is It Another Country? Or a Place To Stow National Problems? A Yankee Journalist Gets Lost and Found in the South"; pp. 20-27, *Columbia Journalism Review*, March/April 2004.

108 Ibid, p. 20.

109 Ibid.

110 Ibid, p. 25.

111 Ibid.

112 H. Brandt Ayers provides a more complete and compelling invitation in "Affirmative Southern Strategy," *Anniston Star*, November 9, 2008.

Index